NVINCIBLE

PAUL BOULOS

BULLETPROOF MINDSET
AND SKILLSET IN THE
FAST-CHANGING WORLD
WHAT DOES IT TAKE?

First published by Paul N.Boulos

978-0-6456542-0-2 | Invincible | Paperback
978-0-6456542-1-9 | Invincible | Ebook

Cover and interior crafted with love by the team at:
www.myebook.online

MYEBOOK
WE EMPOWER AUTHORS

TABLE OF CONTENTS

FOREWORD

Paul,

Congratulations! You are the best, there are no limits,

BY BRIAN TRACY

DEDICATION

This book is dedicated to 'Najib', my grandfather and life mentor.
You were solid as a rock, yet flexible like water, with an unbreakable spirit.
May your soul rest in peace Grandfather.

This book is also dedicated to my daughters, Yulia and Yassma.
You are my lifeblood.

In addition, I would like to dedicate this book to my late sister Paula.
You are watching over us from the heavens.

Finally, it is also dedicated to every person who wants to be self-inspired and sharpen their mindset and life skills, and to everyone who strives to be 'iNVINCIBLE' and have a more meaningful life.

It is dedicated to you, the youth.

ONE BATTLE AT A TIME

PREFACE

THANK YOU.

Thank you for your curiosity.
Thank you for picking up this book.
I hope it changes your life forever.

This book is designed to be short, as the average attention span is short. I have this in mind. It is said that the youth will generally only pay attention for a few seconds. So, I have a few seconds to convince you to listen.

I have spent more than 25 years in the corporate world, managing the top three multinationals in my field at the time. Many perceived my career progression as a big success, especially when I was promoted into senior management at a relatively young age.

I intentionally wanted to start this book with the words 'Thank you'.
I believe that gratitude acts as a foundation of all that is presented in these pages. In fact, there is no way possible that you will achieve and receive before being thankful: thankful for who you are, thankful for what you are worth, and thankful for what you have now. A German theologist, Meister Eckhart once said: 'If the only prayer you say in your life is "thank you," that would suffice.' So, thank you!

My true wish is to transfer my knowledge and life experience over to you to help you be the best version of yourself. I hope that these ideas will assist you as much as they have helped me and thousands of others whose path I have crossed.

This book will bring you, the youth a higher level of awareness of what it takes to survive and thrive in the 21st century.

There is never enough time to do everything we want to achieve. Your generation especially is bombarded with a huge influx of information daily and the speed of life is accelerating rapidly. You are exposed to hundreds if not thousands of messages in a day – or even in just an hour.
Distraction is served on a golden platter.

We have been programmed that we need to succeed. Success has become an overrated idea – an idea that is being portrayed in a generic and superficial materialistic manner.

Being subjected to social media, the youth today form certain archetypes and role models that society idealizes. Those archetypes are not necessarily you. As a result, the times you are living in are competitive and fast.

They can be very tough on occasion. It is almost like being in a race of scarcity where the thinking is:

If you win, I lose, and vice versa.
Instead, you need to make it a journey of abundance.
This can be achieved by harnessing all what you have within you, and by leveraging all what's around you to make it a win-win.

It all starts with you the individual and the youth as you carve your self-concept and your identity.

A JOURNEY OF ABUNDANCE IS ACHIEVED BY HARNESSING ALL WHAT YOU HAVE WITHIN YOU, AND BY LEVERAGING ALL WHAT'S AROUND YOU TO MAKE IT A WIN-WIN.

It all starts with you the individual and the youth as you carve your self-concept and your identity.
What do you stand for?
What are your passions?
What are you going to do in this life?
What are you going to be in this life?

Life is a balance.
You may get far on one track of life, then again you may find out suddenly that you have missed many others and hence you are not self-fulfilled.

It is not possible to do all at once. It is not possible to be everything to everyone. This is why you need to learn how to get ahead and thrive in a more productive and efficient way. You also need to enjoy the journey, and to make the path self-fulfilling.

Remember, there are no half-lived lives and thus no half measures!
Let me repeat that: no half measures.

> **REMEMBER, THERE ARE NO HALF-LIVED LIVES AND THUS NO HALF MEASURES!**

Time does not wait. Not for me, not for you, not for any of us.
You may feel that you are already short on time. You can wish that you had more time. But this is as far as it goes. The truth of the matter is that time does not wait for any of us as we go on our journey. Time only gets faster and faster as if it is slipping out of our hands like running water. You don't have control over time.

You can only get control of your life. You control what you desire.
This happens when you master yourself, your habits. You control your life when you build, learn and perfect the necessary life skills.

Learning these skills and investing in growing yourself is how to truly succeed in this world. Once mastered, these few skills can really make the difference in your life.

I have studied mindset and habits across many walks of life for more than 25 years now. I was inspired by various individuals. From thinkers to teachers, from masters to thought leaders, I have immersed myself in their works, lectures and discussions. Some of them are Brian Tracy (whom I was fortunate to meet and converse with in person), Alan Watts, Dr. Wayne Dyer, Deepak Chopra, Robin Sharma, Ken Robinson, Steve Jobs, Napoleon Hill, Stephen Covey, Edward Debono, Noam Chomsky, Daniel Goleman, Albert Einstein, Bruce Lipton, Anthony Robbins, Ekhart Tolle, Yuval Noah Harari, Marcus Aurelius, Lao-Tzu, and many, many others.

What does it take to survive and thrive in the 21st century?
My search for my own truth and success was a question that I had always asked myself. This question grew even bigger as my two daughters stepped into their teens.

I came to the conclusion that there must be a better way to be iNVINCIBLE in the 21st century. We should not rely on methods that are based on trial and error. I have read hundreds of books and thousands of articles. I have had compelling conversations with many individuals, including business leaders, community leaders, opinion leaders, academics and random strangers from various walks of life. I have analyzed the business I consult.

The findings I made I have synthesized in this book. It is the summation of all my life to date, my personal and professional experience. This book is the result, which I would now like to share with you, so you too can do better, live better and be more self-fulfilled. I want you to be thriving instead of simply surviving in this 21st century.

Looking back, each time I came across a good idea, I tried it out in my own work and personal life. If it worked, I incorporated it into my talks and seminars and taught it to others. After all, as Charles Darwin once said:
'It is not the strongest of the species that survive, nor the most intelligent, but the one most responsive to change.'

Learn those skills. Develop them.
Train them over and over until they become your arsenal. In so doing, you will draw upon them, and they will positively alter the course of your life forever.

LET'S START!

INTRODUCTION

I contemplated a great deal on what to name this book, and in my mind, there was always the word 'YOU', but then again, I really wanted to pass a message to the 'Youth'.

You see, there is no limit to anything except the limits that you have in your mind. To demonstrate this point, we can draw on thousands of examples across the globe where age was never a showstopper and never will be. Colonel Harland David Sanders was 65 years old when he founded KFC. This is an interesting example, as the majority of people retire at his age, as opposed to starting a business.

Even more significant in this example is that he founded it in the era of the Great Depression and a complete economic meltdown. On the extreme end of the stick here is another story that also fulfils the key message I am aiming to pass to you – Michael Phelps' story, the famous Olympic athlete who became, at the age of 15 years and nine months, the youngest swimmer ever to break the world 200-metre butterfly record. Again, what is significant here in this story is that he had anxiety and fear of his face hitting the water! Something he had to overcome to ultimately achieve what he did.

My story is different to yours. Each one of us has our own DNA. Each one of us has a story to tell. Sharing my learnings with you will hopefully help you. At the very least, it should act as a dose of inspiration to assist you to craft your own unique story. You will be equipped with the necessary skills that you require along the way as you craft yours. If you follow the advice and pointers in these pages, you will be truly 'iNVINCIBLE'.

Dr. Wayne Dyer once said:
'Don't die with **your** music still in **you.**'
We all have a song inside ourselves. We need to sing it to the world before leaving this planet. That way, we leave this earth with no regrets.

Isolation, too, can be a killer. In a study done by Harvard University on understanding, researchers wanted to understand how to invest in your best self. They concluded that happiness is all about maintaining good and healthy relationships.

Sadly, far too many people develop a false sense of self. They spend their lives on seemingly important things like career and status. They neglect to care about the things that help them to develop a decent sense of well-being.

Fact is, we are social beings. We need healthy relationships.

Far too often, people regret not having nurtured good relationships. In her book, The Top Five Regrets of the Dying, Bronnie Ware says:

'I wish I'd had the courage to live a life true to myself, not the life others expected of me.
I wish I hadn't worked so hard.
I wish I'd had the courage to express my feelings.
I wish I had stayed in touch with my friends.'

No one was there to tell me all of this as I grew up.
In essence, I wish that I had a mentor when I was in my teens or even in my early twenties – a mentor who could have guided me through the cumulative wisdom of life. Wisdom that I could profit from, instead of having to learn the hard way.

It doesn't have to be done the hard way though. I am here to share and transfer knowledge that I have learned on my journey, hoping that it may help you as you craft your own unique journey. The process of thriving in the 21st century is simple. You start by identifying the necessary skills that you need to thrive – and once you are aware of them, you develop them. **You** actively go to learn and master the competencies.

REPEAT.

Ok, what I meant by repeat here is that the above advice is exactly like brushing your teeth – it is done continuously and on a daily basis. The same goes for building a strong mindset and skillset; it is an ongoing task on **your** journey.

I have spent years balancing between two worlds. I was an educator, lecturing to postgraduate students, and at the same time, I was in the corporate world.
Through this experience, I realized how big the gap is between where the youth are, and the real world.

Today, more than ever, I am compelled to pass this message to the young people so they can narrow this gap and cruise through this century.
Positive change is badly needed across all levels: individual, communal, and worldwide.

We are seeing the rise of unemployment, a major shift in the workplace, and an increase in Artificial Intelligence. The list goes on. **One of the key questions is: How can we grow to be iNVINCIBLE and prosperous while tapping into the new ecosystem and technology advancement without losing purpose or lacking abundance?**

Humanity has so much to offer. I believe in humanity. As a believer in humanity, I believe that the youth is the future. Even more so, I know that the **you**th will create that future.

Instead of being left behind, the youth should therefore be the main driver of good. It is the youth, after all, who will be the voice of change – and who will be carrying the change that is good for our overall benefit.

Remember: You make tomorrow. You contribute to the future more than you think. As the famous Greek philosopher Aristotle once put it:
'The whole is greater than the sum of its parts.' You are not here alone! Each one of you must play your part that ends up contributing to the bigger picture which is humanity.

To me, it all starts with the youth and ends with the youth.

When I say the youth, I mean you as the individual and you as the young man and woman reading this book. You can be in your last years of school, at university, just entering the workplace, or even languishing with unemployment at present. It is you who draw the big picture, and paint the canvas that will become your life.

The first part of this book is therefore about you. More specifically,
it's about the skills that you need regardless of the situation that you're faced with. In the following chapters, I aim to guide you to answer this question: What does it take to be iNVINCIBLE?

Chapter one talks about a major foundational skill, namely: a positive mindset. As Earl Nightingale puts it: 'Your mind is your goldmine.'

Fortunately, we have been given these minds to put to a great use, so if you think negatively, the net result and end outcome will be negative.
The reverse also holds true. If you have a positive mindset, the net outcome of your life endeavors will be positive. Rest assured of that. There is no magic pill you can use as a substitute. You will not wake up tomorrow

thinking positively, if you happen to have a negative mindset. You need to train yourself.

Chapter two is about **self-confidence**. Self-confidence falls under the belief that each one of us is worthy. It needs to be nurtured. There is a beautiful quote for Marcus Garvey that left a great impact on my life. It goes like this:

'If you have no confidence in self, you are twice defeated in the race of life. With confidence, you have won even before you have started.'
The first time I read it, I was only 17 years of age, and it still lives with me to this day of writing it here and sharing it with you.

Note that by confidence, I do not mean arrogance. It is really a thin line between both, with confidence meaning that you remain humble,

while arrogance is inflating your ego and stepping over others.
Confidence comes with the thinking of knowing what knowledge you are able to transfer and serve others with, while arrogance is believing you know it all and you push your ideas and beliefs onto others.

Chapter three is about **clarity**, since without clarity of thinking and clarity of vision, it is impossible to achieve anything or accomplish anything significant.
I refer here in the sub-heading of this chapter to this statement:
'Direction is more important than speed.'

Chapter four is where we delve into **critical thinking**. We go on to tackle what I call the egg and the chicken and the reason why. For perspective, critical thinking is the analysis of available facts, evidence, observations, and arguments to form a judgment. In my view, this is at the heart of what critical thinking is, and why it is so important to our evolution.

The subject is complex; several different definitions exist, which generally include the rational, skeptical, and unbiased analysis or evaluation of factual evidence.

Chapter five is about **communication**, the basic definition of which is the ability to convey or share ideas and feelings effectively. Having spent most of my career in the communication and creative field, this is an important area that we cover, as there is much to be learned here and not just in spoken communication, but more importantly, in what is not being said.

Chapter six is about **imagination.** I will share with you some tips as to how you can grow this skill, and some techniques that were designed by the godfather on this topic, Edward de Bono. As Einstein put it: 'Imagination is more important than knowledge.'

In chapter seven, we discuss **collaboration**, which essentially means you are dealing with others! As such, much can be done when teaming up with other people. The sub-heading to this chapter best expresses my intent with this section: 'Lonely wolves die hard!' Why do it alone if you can collaborate with others, where so much more can be achieved?

In chapter eight, we delve into **connectedness**. Jim Rohn famously said that we are the average of the five people we spend the most time with. We discuss how significant connectedness is and how to choose who to connect with.

Chapter nine is about **resilience.** Here I draw on my grandfather's life experience. Being ready to bounce back comes because of all the previous skills shared and, when nurtured, resilience becomes your second nature. You are then on your way to being **'INVINCIBLE'**.

The second part of the book describes in brief the world we live in today, and from many perspectives. It also helps you answer the question as to how you can plug yourself in it without having to struggle in the rat race.
How can you still find purpose and prosperity while leveraging the technological advancements and the fast-changing world?

We are in the throes of what has been termed the 'Great Reset', and in such a short time. Some of these changes are because of the pandemic and other major shifts that took and are taking place. This gives us yet another reason to be 'iNVINCIBLE' and to choose the life we wish to lead into the future, and create a meaningful journey and existence.
Remember: **there are no half measures.**

REMEMBER:
THERE ARE NO HALF MEASURES.

PART ONE- YOU AND YOURSELF

POSITIVE MINDSET

What you think you become

THINK POSITIVE, LIVE POSITIVE

I remember a very close friend by his famous quote:
'Think positive, live positive.'

He repeated this quote when things went wrong, when things were not looking bright, and when we were faced with hardship.
He always repeated this mantra:
'Think positive, live positive.'

It might seem like a cliché or a gimmick.
The truth is, it is not.

In fact, your mind is an extremely powerful tool. It differentiates us from other beings, as we can translate ideas into reality. Whatever you feed your mind, one way or another it will end up impacting the outcome. Before we go any further, it is always helpful to start with a definition of positive thinking. In Remez Sasson's description: 'Positive thinking is a mental and emotional attitude that focuses on the bright side of life and expects positive results.'

According to many fields, ranging from psychology to business, it becomes evident that your thoughts dictate the results. Hence, came the title, What you think you become. It flows like this:

Your thoughts become your beliefs
Your beliefs become actions
And your actions bring results.

The link between the starting point and the outcomes is clear. There is a direct correlation in this process.

So, if we feed our minds a positive thought, it will lead into shaping a positive belief, hence into a positive action and a positive outcome. The reverse is equally true, so if you choose to think negatively, it is most likely that the outcome you will attract will be negative as well.

THE VICTOR – VICTOR PRINCIPLE

Yes, it is that simple. You choose to be positive.
You choose to be negative.

The choice is yours as to which side you choose to take.

In my coaching sessions to the youth, I always share with them the 'victor–victor' principle from a book titled, *The Oz Principle* by Roger Connors, Tom Smith, and Craig Hickman. The book discusses accountability, leadership, and results.

It explains the mental divide between you and yourself. What you choose to think sets the tone for how you interact with the world. According to these authors, there are two types of people: The victors, and the victims.

On one hand, victors fuel their thoughts with the mentality of 'abundance'. It is always a win-win situation with victors. On the other, victims fuel their thoughts with a 'scarcity' mentality, which leads to a win-lose.

WE LIVE IN AN ABUNDANT UNIVERSE. YOU ARE PART OF THIS ABUNDANCE!

You are born to be living by choice, not by obligation. Victors live by choice, while victims live by obligation.

Victors have nothing to prove to others. They have a positive outlook. They are responsible. They take ownership. They have a vision for excellence. Victims, on the other hand, delve into blaming others.

They blame circumstances. They love to create excuses. They think negatively. They live in denial, as they are stuck in the scarcity mentality.

Being a victor does not mean that life will not throw challenges at you. Most certainly, life will always throw challenges at you. The key is how you choose to respond.

LIFE WILL ALWAYS THROW CHALLENGES AT YOU. THE KEY IS HOW YOU CHOOSE TO RESPOND.

You may not have control of the event itself, but always you get to choose how you wish to respond. Avis J. Williams, author of *The Psychic Mind* said: 'We can't control everything that happens to us, but we can control how we respond to things we can't control.'

This is strongly linked to having a positive mindset. Building a positive mindset allows you to choose better and create more positive responses to life's events. Positive responses make the future kinder.

This book will not prevent bad things from happening. Rather, it will help to guide you through a well-tried recipe that allows you to face the many challenges in the coming decade. It outlines how you can be well equipped to navigate through them.

STOIC PHILOSOPHY

One of the great thinkers who inspired my journey was Marcus Aurelius.

Besides his relative success as being a great military general and a Roman emperor, he is also best known as a Stoic philosopher. He truly attempted to live his philosophy. He stressed the power of the mind, our thoughts, and how they can dictate the outcome.

Aurelius became famous for the Meditations, a collection of his deliberations. He subscribed to the Stoic school of thought.

He said: 'You have power over your mind – not outside events. Realize this, and you will find strength.'

Many great men and women, philosophers, and leaders throughout the history of humankind realized how important it is to have a positive mindset, and each expressed it in their own way.

Before delving deeper into positive mindset, let's first understand what a mindset is and why it matters when acquiring the necessary skills to thrive in the coming decade.

WHAT IS MINDSET?

No doubt you have come across this word 'mindset' a lot. At first, it may appear vague or blurry.
Let's explore it . . .

The subject of mindset has been talked about extensively in behavioral research. There are many educators, authors, and researchers who have addressed it. They range from the field of psychology to sociology and behavioral science.

According to the educator and author Kendra Cherry, a mindset refers to how you view your intelligence and talent and other traits. There are two types of mindsets: fixed or changeable. She describes them as follows:

1. The fixed mindset are the ones who believe that their qualities and abilities are fixed.

2. The growth mindset are those who believe that their abilities can be developed and strengthened by way of commitment and consistent work.

In his book, *Maximum Achievement*, Brian Tracy speaks of the seven laws of mental mastery. Among these laws, the 'Law of belief' sticks out.
It says: 'Whatever you believe, with feeling, becomes your reality.'

This law led to one of Brian's signature quotes: 'You become what you think about most of the time.'

He lists other laws: The Law of self-control, Law of cause and effect, Law of belief, Law of expectations, Law of attraction, Law of correspondence, and the Law of mental equivalency.

Google them. Study them. Make them a part of who you are.

I once met Brian in person and received a personal dedication that says: 'Paul, congratulations! You are the best, there are no limits.'

Apply these short words to you. They are as true for you as they are for me. You are the best. There are no limits whatsoever. The only limits are those that you place on yourself, the limits that you actively keep in your own mind. Hence, all starts with mindset.

In my corporate career, I was fortunate to have worked with the top three global corporations in my field. When Leo Burnett Worldwide, an American advertising company called us for training sessions on brand planning and consumer dynamics, they had already built an entire brand planning system and it was called 'The brand belief system'.

It all starts with belief. Belief reflects what goes on inside the organization. What goes inside gets reflected to the outside world and how the organization connects and builds affinity with consumers.

WHY IS MINDSET IMPORTANT?

Mindsets can be changed. Thank God!

Research shows that mindset and beliefs can be altered. In my career in marketing and advertising, we faced many brands with negative perception. This is a serious problem when you are a business and want your customers to trust you with their money.

We used to be thankful that perceptions can be changed over time. Otherwise, we would be out of business. All ties back together. You get to choose what mindset you wish to have: a fixed mindset, or a growth mindset?

Some questions to consider when evaluating your own mindset, as put by Kendra Cherry, are as follows:

1.People have a certain amount of intelligence, and there isn't any way to change it.

2. No matter who you are, there isn't much you can do to improve your basic abilities and personality.

3.People are capable of changing who they are.

4.You can learn new things and improve your intelligence.

5.People either have particular talents, or they don't. You can't just acquire talent for things such as music, writing, art, or athletics.

6.Studying, working hard, and practicing new skills are all ways to develop new talents and abilities.

Steven Covey also highlights the importance of choices because of mindset, and he says: 'But until a person can say deeply and honestly, "I am what I am today because of the choices I made yesterday," that person cannot say, "I choose otherwise."

MY TWO CENTS

As you can see, I am not dwelling on the concept of 'success'.
In my view, success is overrated.
Success can mean different things to different people.

Success can be largely associated with material wealth and belongings.
But digging deeper, success is way more than this.

This section can best be summed up by what Joan of Arc once said:
'All battles are first won or lost, in the mind.'
It all starts with **you** and ends with **you.**

IT ALL STARTS WITH YOU AND ENDS WITH YOU.

CONFIDENCE: YOU ARE WORTHY

YOU WILL WIN THE RACE OF LIFE

'If you have no confidence in self, you are twice defeated in the race of life. With confidence, you have won even before you have started.'

This is a quote said by Orator and Activist Marcus Garvey.
When I was 17 years of age, I came across this statement, and I immediately identified with it.

Each time I read it, it had more meaning to it and to me. As a teenager, we used to hang posters in our rooms to display pictures of our idols and archetypes.

This statement had its share in my room space. I hung it on my ceiling, where it grew much bigger in my mind and headspace. I stuck it on the ceiling right above my head, so it was the last thing I read before I slept every night.

Please take a moment and pause while you read it and reflect on it.

YOUR PURPOSE GOES WAY BEYOND YOUR EDUCATION

It all starts with **you.**
It all ends with **you.**
Yes, that is where it all starts and ends.

You can choose to live your life sleeping, or you can choose to live it while you are fully awake.
Literally and laterally.

So, are you still sleeping? Or are you waking up?

Are you ready to wake up? If so, how serious are you about it? (What I meant here by awake, is being aware of your own self, existence, why are you here, and what have you come to be? To do?) And how are you going to create meaning to your life and the life of others whom you may cross on your path?

Remember: You are part of this universe. You are in motion. Just like a wave in the ocean, heading to its ultimate destination, the motion is there.
You are not a puppet that life pushes around.

On the contrary, the real you, deep down is the whole universe. **You exist.**

So, if you exist then you must have a meaningful existence.

Why just exist without meaning?

It is like sleeping without waking up!

If you exist, then you are awake. If you are awake, then you must have a better idea about the real you.

Your purpose goes way beyond your education.

You are an extraordinarily complex creature, so focus on how you think and act. Think about the things that you do without being educated about. Like walking, talking, or seeing.

A small act of believing in oneself can be a big act of faith that allows you to accomplish many outcomes without being fearful, just like the examples given before.

Walk in faith, and things will walk with you and around you.

> **YOUR PURPOSE GOES WAY BEYOND YOUR EDUCATION.**

YOU ARE WORTH SOMETHING

The following is inspired from Alan Watts' speech, The Real You:
You are worth something!
Self-worth is especially important when discussing confidence.

The dictionary defines self-worth as 'the sense of one's own value or worth as a person.'

However, there are many ways for a person to value themselves and assess their worth as a human being. Some of these are more psychologically beneficial than others.

In this section, we discuss the value of true self-worth.
We also discuss how to build your sense of self-worth and why so many of us lack a feeling of worthiness.

YOU KNOW WHO YOU ARE

Dr. Robert Firestone is the author of several books, one of which is *The Self Under Siege.*

He believes that self-worth should be less about measuring yourself based on external actions and more about valuing your inherent worth as a person.

In other words, self-worth is about who you are, not about what you do.

SELF-WORTH IS ABOUT WHO YOU ARE, NOT ABOUT WHAT YOU DO

The first step in building self-worth is to stop comparing yourself to others. When you find yourself doing so, you need to challenge your inner voice.

Our inner voice can be negative sometimes. That is why we need to challenge our inner critic.
We need to begin to see ourselves for who we really are.
We shouldn't be focusing on just the negative.
When we challenge ourselves in a positive way, we begin to understand and appreciate our own feelings, thoughts, desires, and values.

YOU ARE LOVING, CURIOUS, OPEN AND ACCEPTING

A true sense of self-worth can be fostered by practicing self-compassion.

Dr. Kristin Neff, who has a doctorate in studying moral development, has defined self-compassion as the practice of treating yourself with the same kindness as you would treat a friend. She breaks down self-compassion as being composed of three main elements as follows: 1. Self-kindness, 2. Common Humanity and 3. Mindfulness.

This involves the COAL attitude as Dr. Dan Siegel puts it. The COAL attitude entails being Curious, Open, Accepting and Loving towards yourself and your experiences.

Dr. Siegel is a clinical professor in psychiatry and has done a great deal of research on the topic of mindful awareness.

A more practical approach to COAL would be being a student of life itself, open to learn and learning which comes in many different ways and forms, not just being in school in a formal system.

YOU ARE ACTIVE

Add meaning to your life by being active, and taking part in activities that you feel are important. This is another great way to build self-worth.

People find meaning in many ways. Some people defend a cause. Others devote their lives to art and aesthetics. It doesn't matter what way you choose to add meaning to your life. **You** need merely to choose something you enjoy, and then immerse yourself in it. This act boosts your self-worth.

Dr. Jennifer Crocker suggests that you find a goal that is bigger than the self. The building of self-worth is directly connected to discovering your purpose and acting on it.

For example, if your passion is all about art, then you pursue that and with time this becomes a goal larger than life and creates meaning to you, rather than being stuck in a 9 to 5 job doing a mundane type of work that does not answer or honor your passion.

Thus, by pursuing activities that are meaningful to you and acting in line with your own personal beliefs, you can develop your sense of yourself as a worthwhile person in the world even further.

YOU ARE SELF-CONFIDENT

Self-confidence.

We get bombarded by this word.

But really, what is self-confidence?
One answer comes from the Counseling Center of the University of South Florida. They defined self-confidence as an attitude about your skills and abilities. It means you accept and trust yourself. You have a sense of control in your life.

You know your strengths well.

You know your weaknesses well.
You know them so well that you have a positive view of yourself.
You set realistic expectations and goals.
You communicate assertively.
You can handle criticism.

Low self-confidence, on the other hand, might result in a variety of problems.
It might make you feel full of self-doubt.
You might be passive or submissive as a result.
You may have difficulty trusting others.
You may feel inferior, unloved, or be sensitive to criticism.

Feeling confident in yourself might depend on the situation. For instance, you can feel greatly confident in some areas, such as academics, but lack confidence in others, like relationships.

Having high or low self-confidence is rarely related to your actual abilities. It is mostly based on your perceptions.

Perceptions are the way you think about yourself, and these thoughts can be flawed.
Let this concept sink in:

YOUR PERCEPTION DETERMINES YOUR CONFIDENCE.

Here is a list of actions that increase your self-confidence:

- Recognize and emphasize your strengths. Reward and praise yourself for your efforts and progress.

- When you stumble on an obstacle, treat yourself with kindness and compassion. Don't dwell on failure.

- Set realistic and achievable goals. Do not expect perfection; it is impossible to be perfect in every aspect of life.

- Slow down when you are feeling intense emotions and think logically about the situation.

- Challenge any assumptions you make about yourself, people, and situations.

- Recognize that past negative life experiences do not dictate your future.

- Express your feelings, beliefs and needs directly and respectfully.

- Learn to say no to unreasonable requests. Individual counseling can also help increase your self-confidence if you require more help.

Read this list five times.
Read it slowly.
Let it sink in.

Self-confidence is a combination of a state of mind and a strong feeling of self-belief.

Self-confidence is less something one uses, and far more something that one possesses, especially in one's personal judgment, power, and ability.

Self-confidence comes from your inside. It is that voice that gives you a boost to do something you fear.

In the 21st century, the race of life has become much more competitive. There is no place for those who lack self-confidence, because there is no shortage of good talent now.
The competition is high.

A great number of people are achieving their goals using confidence as a ladder. For the **you**th especially, confidence plays a key aspect in life.
It extends way beyond the school and university years.

In a nutshell, with higher confidence levels, you will have far greater chances for success.

YOU ARE YOU, REGARDLESS OF THE TITLE YOU WEAR

Your self-worth is not defined by your title.

Let me tell **you** a story.

I have worked in more than nine corporations over a 25-year period.
In each company, I held a certain position and role.
In some instances, I held more than one role in one given company.

Each time I left a certain company, I would keep my business card as a souvenir. Over time, I collected many of these business cards.

Looking at these cards today, you can see various company names and various titles, but only one name, my name.

At some point, I was once made redundant.
I stayed home for a more than two months before finding another opportunity.
At that point, I confirmed to myself what I always knew:
Self-worth is not defined by a title printed on a business card, or by what you do for a living.

> **SELF-WORTH IS NOT DEFINED BY A TITLE PRINTED ON A BUSINESS CARD, OR BY WHAT YOU DO FOR A LIVING.**

Mahatma Gandhi inspired the world.
In a racist environment, he was called a 'little brown man' who 'held no official office and had no official title'!
Yet Mahatma Gandhi managed to inspire – and even change – the world.

WHO ARE YOU?

I used to find it very superficial when going out to socialize. The very first thing people would typically ask you after saying hello is:
What do you do?

A better question would be:
How are you?

While the greatest question is:
Who are **you**, and what makes **you** tick?

Your self-worth is not defined by what you do.
It is defined by answering these questions to yourself:
Who are you?
Why are **you** here?
What do **you** love to do?

Every year, I used to go on a recruitment tour to interview fresh graduates.
I would often start with the same question:
How would you describe yourself in a few short words?

I used to get the generic answer of these young people. Graduates with high GPA scores telling me their name, their age, and, what they studied!

They totally missed the point.
They were misguided in their upbringing about the definition of self-worth!

Due to social stigma, we condition ourselves and our kids to define self-worth materialistically. And yet, we are so much more than that.

ANSWER ME: WHO ARE YOU?

Write down the answer to this question: Who are you?
Hint: Don't answer with your degrees or your job position.

MEDITATION: I AM A PURE SPIRIT

I would like to share with you a beautiful meditation.

I learned it a few years back from the book *Three Magic Words* by Uell Stanley Andersen. It helped me greatly in reminding me of my worth.

It became a good reference for dusting off any lack of confidence that I might feel.

I usually listen to it before I sleep as my subconscious mind is getting ready to kick off for the night.

Please read it slowly and repeat it:
'I know that I am pure spirit, that I always have been, and that I always will be. There is inside me a place of confidence and quietness and security where

all things are known and understood. This is the Universal Mind, God, of which I am a part of, and which responds to me as I ask of it.

This Universal Mind knows the answer to all my problems, and even now the answers are speeding their way to me.

I needn't struggle for them; I needn't worry or strive for them. When the time comes, the answers will be there. I give my problems to the great mind of God; I let go of them, confident that the correct answers will return to me when they are needed.

Through the great law of attraction, everything in life that I need for my work and fulfillment will come to me. It is not necessary that I strain about this – only believe. For in the strength of my belief, my faith will make it so. I see the hand of divine intelligence all about me, in the flower, the tree, the brook and the meadow.

I know that the intelligence that created all these things is in me and around me and that I can call upon it for my slightest need. I know that my body is a manifestation of pure spirit and that spirit is perfect; therefore, my body is perfect also. I enjoy life, for each day brings a constant demonstration of the power and wonder of the universe and myself. I am confident. I am serene. I am sure.

*No matter what obstacle or undesirable circumstance crosses my path,
I refuse to accept it, for it is nothing but illusion. There can be no obstacle or undesirable circumstance to the mind of God, which is in me, and around me, and serves me now.'*

CLARITY: DIRECTION IS MORE IMPORTANT THAN SPEED

MARCUS AURELIUS: CLARITY

Marcus Aurelius led one of the most powerful empires in history.

His key trait was his ability to leverage the clarity of his mind. This is because, the more **you** are aware, the more **you** can accomplish, and the more possibilities lie ahead of **you.**

Aurelius demonstrated to us that the ability to think clearly is a keystone advantage. He also demonstrated that it can be acquired like any other skill.

While drawn to philosophy, Aurelius was particularly interested in Stoicism. Stoicism is based on the notion that behaviors, not thoughts or words, should define virtue.

The clearest image of Aurelius is painted through a series of notes he wrote to himself, known as *Meditations*.

Meditations is a timeless manual for living a balanced life and achieving clarity of mind. It describes how Aurelius saw the world as it was,
rather than as he hoped it would be.

Every day, we are bombarded with external events. If we were to internalize each one of these incidents, we would not be able to function properly.

Our minds will be cluttered, and hence lack clarity.

In his book, Aurelius pointed out three ways to clear this clutter and achieve clarity.

LOOK BEYOND WHAT YOU LITERALLY SEE

Aurelius pointed out the value of looking beyond what we intuitively see on the surface in daily life to better understand the world.

> **'NOTHING HAS SUCH POWER TO BROADEN THE MIND AS THE ABILITY TO INVESTIGATE SYSTEMATICALLY AND TRULY ALL THAT COMES UNDER THY OBSERVATION IN LIFE.'**
> **- MARCUS AURELIUS**

THE FLY ON THE WALL

Aurelius had a profound ability to step away from his own mind and see the world and himself without emotional attachment.
It helps explain the depth of his insight.

Stepping away is a powerful tool.
It assists us to separate our thoughts from our feelings. When our thoughts are clouded by feelings such as anger, we narrow down our scope.
This results in hasty judgments.

When I was in the process of obtaining my life coaching certifications, we were given a task to step outside of ourselves.
Our task was that we needed to role play and be a fly on the wall.

How does it see the room?
Does it care – and if so, why?

EMPTY YOUR MIND

Aurelius did not write his meditations for anyone to read.
He wrote them for himself.

By all accounts, it appears to be a very personal journal.
There is not much coherence or structure to how it's presented.
His purpose for writing was not necessarily to share his wisdom.

Rather, it was for him to clear out and organize his own mind. This was a therapeutic exercise, which each one of us needs to do to declutter our mind. My advice to you is therefore this: Journal your days, and then read your journals.

Declutter your mind with writing.

Alternatively, you can find a routine exercise that you love to do, an exercise that helps you to clear your mind. Practice it. Declutter your thinking.
I personally use writing.

This fact is greatly supported by behavioral research and science.
Examples of routines used by my own students include:
- nature walks
- sport
- gardening

- playing your favorite musical instrument
- stargazing, etc.

The human mind is extremely noisy.

It is therefore important that **you** create a routine that allows **you** to clear it up. In so doing, it becomes less noisy, and **you** are able to perceive more clearly.

SIXTY THOUSAND THOUGHTS, FILTER THEM!

Esteemed neuroscientist and philosopher, Dr. Deepak Chopra confirms that the human mind averages around 60,000 to 80,000 thoughts per day. Can you imagine the significance of such number?

If we wrote down every thought that passed through our minds as a line, we would have enough text to fill a library as large as Shakespeare's bibliography in just two days!
It's like watching a monitor of a terribly busy airport.

Scientists and research also show that not all these thoughts are necessarily positive or important!

To think and perceive clearly, you therefore need to filter out the noise.

TO THINK AND PERCEIVE CLEARLY, YOU NEED TO FILTER OUT THE NOISE.

KEY DETERMINING LIFE QUESTIONS

Many years ago, I listened to a speech by Brian Tracy, titled: *Power of Clarity*. It was a game changer in my life. I recall listening to it almost daily as I drove my car to work and back.
I listened to it repeatedly.

It challenges you to answer multiple, key determining life questions, which I elaborate on below. He asks them, and you must answer them.

Today, I am a Life Coach, Business Coach and Business Consultant/Advisor, and I coach my clients exactly this. I ask them determining life questions.

The clarity module put together by Brian takes you through a journey of knowing yourself. You identify your starting point, allowing you to declutter by eliminating what is not important, what is irrelevant and what is not.

Then, it offers you the chance to construct your own personal and strategic plan. Brian sums this up in what he calls the eight foundational strategic questions. **You** need to answer those questions, yourself.

By so doing, it provides you clarity regarding your quest for an ideal career, business and, more broadly, life.

I reserved a part for each question in the pages to follow.
Take your time while answering.

VALUES

What are the values, virtues, qualities, and traits that are most important to **you** in your life, business, and career?

Some examples of an indicator of values could be: freedom, family, nature lover, integrity, serving others, etc.

VISION

If your life (business, career, personal, etc.) was perfect five years from today, what would it look like?

MISSION

Based on your values and vision, how specifically do **you** achieve your vision?

PURPOSE

What is the purpose of your life, business, and career?

All truly successful entrepreneurs have an overarching purpose to their business, namely, a genuine desire to serve others through their lives and hence through what they do. Elon Musk is a great example of such entrepreneurs who are driven by purpose.

In my opinion, when it comes to building purpose-driven brands, Elon Musk is something of a pioneer. Be it with his electric car company, Tesla, or his aerospace manufacturing business, SpaceX, it really rotates around helping humanity.

The mission statement of Tesla, for example, starts like this: *'to accelerate the advent of sustainable transport...'*

Purpose-driven people, entrepreneurs, and companies are defined beyond their product and or service. Instead, they tend to act with a far-reaching footprint that creates a positive impact on humanity.

GOALS

What specific goals must **you** achieve to fulfill your ideal future vision in your life, business, and career? Please remember that goals are neither dreams nor wishes; goals are specific, time bound and measurable.

KNOWLEDGE AND SKILLS

In what areas will **you** have to excel in the future to achieve your goals and fulfill your vision?

Hint: Part 2 of this book helps you answer this question.

HABITS

What specific habits of thoughts and actions will **you** need to practice to become the person who can achieve the goals that you have set for yourself? Here you can refer to a couple of my most favorite books, namely: *Atomic Habits* by James Clear and *The 7 Habits of Highly Effective People* by Stephen Covey.

In his book, James Clear focuses his work on guiding **you** to breaking bad behaviors and adopting good ones, highlighting the importance of how small, incremental, everyday routines compound into massive, positive change over time.

On the other hand, Stephen Covey takes a more straightforward approach of describing the seven habits that are believed to serve as a golden recipe for you to lead a more powerful and effective way of being.

DAILY ACTIVITIES

What specific activities will you have to engage in each day to assure that **you** become the person **you** want to be and achieve the goals **you** want to achieve? Being iNVINCIBLE is not an exception to this rule of daily habits.

The best analogy that comes to my mind here is that this daily and continuous process runs exactly like your daily hygiene of brushing your teeth.

THINKING ON PAPER

I did this exercise at age 29. I was compelled to think deep, and to scratch beyond the surface.
I wanted to articulate:

What is my vision, mission, and purpose?
Why am I here?
What am I set to do?
And what do I stand for?

To navigate this complexity, I used paper to think.
Thinking on paper seems so easy as a task and perhaps we undervalue it. But when done, it becomes exceedingly powerful. **You** believe in what you wrote and why you wrote it in the first place.
It takes another dimension of existing beyond just your imagination and cuts through the clutter.

SELF-MASTERY

Robin Sharma, in many of his inspiring talks and speeches refers to the subject of clarity and he says: 'Clarity breeds mastery.'

Lao Tzu, the Chinese philosopher and writer often referred to self-mastery and emphasized its importance by saying: 'Mastering others is strength, mastering yourself is true power.'

LESS IS MORE

Rolf Dobelli in his book, *The Art of Thinking Clearly*, articulates that all we need is less irrationality in the way we think. Some of them are psychological, others are logical. Some are social and are supported by many examples to bring each thinking move to life and make it easy to digest.

I refer to it here since it helps in demonstrating the point about clarity. You can think more with clarity and improve your clarity of thought by going through these moves he highlighted.

When working in the creative field, we used to do high-level pitches to clients. We used to map out the brands' attributes (functional, emotional, etc.) and how these benefits relate to potential customers and clients. These presentations would sometimes reach well over 300 slides.

One of the lessons that I learned during pitching was the 'less is more' principle which Dobelli refers to in his book.

Before learning about this principle, we believed that the more information we put in the presentation the better the chance we had of winning it.
Then comes the Western school of thought in the creative business which taught me that it is quite the opposite.
The less **you** say is really the more **you** say.
Using the example of building affinity between brands and consumers, the more choices and variety you offer, the more confusion there will be.
I know this may sound paradoxical, so let me explain.

'Less is more' is the idea that if **you** present somebody with too many choices, it tends to waste a lot of their time, and may even reduce the quality of their life.

Dobelli refers to the work of psychologist Barry Schwartz. He concluded that generally, the increased number of choices will lead us to make poorer choices than if we had fewer to choose between.

Think about this.
'Less is more' also applies to your thoughts and your mind and the way you think.

To put this into a more concrete example, when faced with a certain issue and you are about to make a decision, list down the facts, evaluate the pros and cons, and aim to be rational and less emotional about the subject.

EXPLORE

Remember: Direction is more important than speed.

What is the point of you running around like a headless chicken, with no clue of where are **you** heading and why?

I am not saying here that you should be born with all the answers.
Most certainly not.
In fact, I am an advocate of the expansive thinking that the youth go through in their teens and twenties, especially when it comes to exploring to find their passions.

If I was to sum up all my thoughts in one word to the young people of today, I would say to them **explore.**

This is the best time to learn and make mistakes, to discover and try out new experiences.
Do it now.
Don't wake up at 50 thinking: 'I wish I had.'
Don't let your last words be: 'If only I had done so.'

DECLUTTER: URGENT–IMPORTANT MATRIX

Throughout my coaching sessions, I always refer to the Urgent–Important Matrix.

This is a simple but effective tool for prioritizing your to-do list based on the level of urgency and importance of each task.

It is one of the easiest time management strategies to implement.

Use it as **you** declutter your mind and realize what is important and what is not.

To help **you** put this in perspective: How many times do **you** hear the word 'urgent' every day?

Looking back at the corporate world, almost everything had the word 'urgent' embedded in it.

Nearly every conversation included the word 'urgent'.
Nearly every job was 'urgent'.
Nearly every correspondence incorporated the word 'urgent'.

The very first thing I always did with my teams was ask them why it was urgent. I used to do this with my clients, suppliers, and even my superiors.

This is a simple method to assess whether things are actually 'urgent'.
In most cases, whatever was labelled as urgent, was not!

Urgency has to do with speed, which is why I said direction is more important than speed.

I am not saying that some things or events can't be urgent. I am just asking **you** to always make sure you check the direction, as in your internal compass that guides **you** to what counts and matters most to **you** and your well-being.

MY TWO CENTS

You are a divine creation of the creator.
You are a perfect example of Higher Intelligence.

Don't spend your entire life living for the sake of living.
Don't do things because '**you** have to'.

The truth is that you and I both know that **you** are not obliged at all.
You always have a choice. **You** decide whether you will live by choice or by obligation.

Living by obligation leads in many instances to a fast and unfulfilled life.
A life where time passes and passes ever faster.

If **you** choose to live by obligation, most likely **you** will be waiting for that pay cheque like most people do.

Living by choice, on the other hand, mirrors the divine intelligence.
You have a direction to a more fulfilled and meaningful life.
I wish I knew what I know today when I was in my teens. What I mean by this, is knowing what counts and what doesn't, what is meaningful and what is not, and what serves my higher purpose.

CRITICAL THINKING: THE EGG, THE CHICKEN, & THE REASON WHY?

CRITICAL THINKING

What does critical thinking mean?

The Oxford Dictionary explains it as follows:

Critical thinking is 'the process of analyzing information in order to make a logical decision about the extent to which you believe something to be true or false'.

Let's break up this definition.

You analyze the information that you get. Analysis helps

you make sense of the information you have.

You make an educated decision, based on your analysis.

Critical thinking is a mix between logic, hard facts, mathematics, reasoning, and philosophy.

PROPEL YOUR ANALYSES BY YOUR INSTINCT

In his book, *Thinking, Fast and Slow,* Daniel Kahneman addresses head-on the psychological biases of most people.

The book summarizes the psychological research on unreliable thinking patterns which all of us are prone to.

He describes patterns of thought as using either 'System One' or 'System Two'.

System One is the fast, intuitive, emotional response to situations where we jump to a conclusion very quickly without thinking about it.

System Two is more analytical and conscious. Because it's methodical and deliberative, it is a slower and more logical process, which is much more energy consuming. System Two is when we stop and think.

The problem is that we typically rely on System One and are often wrong as a result. We forget about System Two.

It is within this framework that much of his analysis is set.

In my view, I believe that we are clearly a combination of both systems.

The mix of these two sets of thought systems differs from one person to another and from one situation to the next.

CRITICAL THINKING AND EDUCATION

The link between critical thinking and education is obvious.

You cannot learn well without thinking well.

YOU CANNOT LEARN WELL WITHOUT THINKING WELL.

Critical thinking contributes to your success in general, and on how you go about living your life. Critical thinking determines the quality of the decisions and actions **you** end up making based on the quality of your thinking.

IT'S NOT WHAT YOU THINK, IT'S HOW YOU THINK IT

In a research study conducted by the University of Oregon, Professor David T. Conley found that 'habits of mind' such as 'analysis, interpretation, precision and accuracy, problem solving, and reasoning' can be as or more important than content knowledge in determining success in college courses.

Learning how to think in a critical manner and having the ability to solve problems effectively are vital skills that the **you**th require for the future.

Learning this skill will allow you to develop other skills.
Skills such as a higher level of concentration, deeper analytical abilities, and improved thought processing.

In today's world, you as the youth must be active critical thinkers.
You need to compare evidence, evaluate competing claims, and make sensible decisions.

FAST IS FASTER

In the 21st century, you will be faced with a vast array of information regarding almost every area of your life. **You** will be required to make fast decisions and to act quickly at times.

We are witnessing a new kind of living in a fast-changing world.
The list goes on: global warming, pandemics, wars, economic instability, the rise in Artificial Intelligence, remote work together with the overall workplace environment, and even the way education is being conducted.

In summary, we are seeing a great shift moving from the physical world as we knew it into the virtual. As the **you**th, you are required to equip yourselves and master this key skill of being able to tackle problems head-on. Today, **you** need to be able to find solutions for yourself in navigating this rapidly changing environment.

In a span of around just seven years, the **you**th between the ages of 17 and 24 go through major shifts in their lives. They transition from home, then school into university or other tertiary education institution if they are able, and then the workplace.

From being financially and emotionally dependent on their parents to being on their own.

They wake up one morning into a new reality, and find themselves floating in this world. A world that is extremely competitive. A world that has little in common with what they have learned in the past.

The environment is not just fast, it's faster than ever!

Critical thinking can be of help.
This skill will serve **you** in your personal life and quality of relationships.
It will also serve you with the work you do.

Regardless of whether you will be working from home or doing freelance work or even full-time work, **you** will still need to interact with superiors, customers, suppliers, etc.

You will still need to create new products and are expected to improve services.

EDUCATION IS RIPE FOR DISRUPTION

Following on from the above, the problem is that our entire education system has been constructed based on how people, governments, and industry thought the world ought to be after World War II. This may seem like an outdated world view and history, however, it is the education system that is outdated, in all aspects of the word.

Creating **you**rself and the future certainly requires a new way of thinking. For this, **you** also need to build a different type of skillset.

Sir Ken Robinson articulated this point very well in his speech, How to create a *culture for valuable learning.* He said at the annual Big Picture Learning conference that, 'If you design a system to do something, don't be surprised if it does it.'

He went on to describe the two pillars of the current system: conformity and compliance. These pillars undermine the sincere efforts of educators and parents to equip children with the confidence to enter the world on their own terms.

Being subjected to conformity and compliance will only limit your mind and your critical thinking ability. It conditions you over time to behave like most people around – i.e. to conform. As a result, your critical thinking skill dwindles with time.

THE FINNISH GOVERNMENT: ADVANCES IN EDUCATION

In education ranking by countries, Finland is one of the most advanced. According to the World Economic Forum's Global Competitive Study, Finland is ranked as having the most well-developed education system in the world.

They are changing the way education will be delivered.
No more scheduled lectures.
No more classrooms.
No more rigid curricula.
They aren't letting education get in the way of learning.

MANAGING THE DUMPS OF INFORMATION

The World Economic Forum reviewed labor market trends and identified skills that employees will need to thrive in the new technical economy.

Guess what, critical thinking was identified as one of those key skills.

In this age of personal bias and varied opinions, critical thinkers are needed more than ever. They are the ones who challenge others' biases and illogical thinking. They bring value to the workplace. More importantly, they bring value to the world at large.

A critical thinker is able to think differently about a situation.
A critical thinker gathers information and develops new ways of understanding.

COURAGE TO THINK

Think of situations where you might have been able to challenge someone to look at a problem in a different way, with a new eye.

One of the pillars behind the success of Netflix is their company culture. If you review their culture deck, you will quickly realize how important it is to acquire and build the skill of critical thinking.

They label it as 'judgment' and 'courage' under their well-crafted culture deck of 'freedom' and 'responsibility'.

THE PRESENT IS DIFFERENT TO THE PAST, THE FUTURE IS DIFFERENT TO THE PRESENT

In his book titled *Factfulness – Ten Reasons We're Wrong About The World – And Why Things Are Better Than You Think,* Hans Rosling, a Swedish statistician and physician addressed this topic.

He also addressed it in his TED talks.

Rosling demonstrates the importance of data and facts, and how we interpret the facts that we have available. He shows the importance of not just assuming that you know, based on how things are now.

He also drives the point that pessimists tend not to notice changes for the better.

His core message from this book is that people assume that the present is like the past. For example, when people have learnt something about the state of world poverty, they often neglect to take a second look.

They neglect to see the direction in which things are moving, and the speed with which things are changing for the better.

You will always get the chance to not assume that the present will be like the past.

You also have the awareness to stop and observe the direction in which things are moving and at what speed things are changing.

You don't have to know the answers in the immediate moment. But at least, you now have the chance to ask yourself these questions.

You can challenge yourself and others in a positive way, seeking better answers that are fact based.

YOU WILL ALWAYS GET THE CHANCE TO NOT ASSUME THAT THE PRESENT WILL BE LIKE THE PAST.

BEING CRITICAL

In my coaching practice, I carry out behavioral assessments for my clients before coaching them. Some of them are more detail oriented, while others are more compliant or score higher on influence.

This does not mean you are required to be an expert statistician to observe and make sense of the facts that are presented before you. Rather, **you** need to avoid accepting facts as is and taking them at face value.

Rosling's book offers you a good invitation to seek better and more intelligent answers about facts. I strongly suggest that you read it.

Critical thinking is now being looked at as a key skill for everyone.
It is not a special skill for the gifted.

The significance of thinking critically is paramount. It is necessary for everyone, especially in today's world.

WHAT IS SUCCESS? REALLY

When wearing the hat of critical thinking, you will automatically start to question the more fundamental truths about various concepts.

You will question ideas that were either overrated or undervalued, if not simply ignored. One overrated idea is the concept of success and failure.

So, what is success? Really.

SO, WHAT DOES SUCCESS REALLY MEAN, TO YOU?

I am sure that by now, **you** have heard the word success a million times, as if there is one definition to it.

You've heard of success as if it only has a single recipe.

For example, one of the main misconceptions of success is greatly linked to material success. Agreed, you might be doing great on the material and money level, but many other aspects of your life might not be doing well at all – and is that considered to be success? When looking at success, one cannot discount the overall wheel of life and ignore the well-being of a person.

Well, to start with, success is very relative to each one of us.
Success to **you**, your sister, brother, father, friend, neighbor will mean something totally different.

Same thing goes for failure!
We are so programmed to look at failure as a taboo.
We are used to thinking that failure is something that should not be discussed.

In my view, most of the real lessons I learned did not stem from success. They came from failure.

> **MOST OF THE REAL LESSONS I LEARNED DID NOT STEM FROM SUCCESS. THEY CAME FROM FAILURE.**

In my life, I had my fair share of so-called failures. Each setback was a great place to learn the best lessons that I needed to learn at the time.

Nelson Mandela once said:
'I never lose. I either win or learn.'

This is the very same concept that we go through in life.
To put it in a more concrete example, when **you** look at any sport, **you** have two opponents and then you have a score, hence a winner and a loser. But if **you** really were to think of it, is the winner really the winner? And is the loser really the loser? What if the loser learns the most from their loss and the winner learns little from their win?

There is a saying that goes along the lines of, 'Nothing is ever lost, it is transformed.'

LEARN FROM FAILURES

In his book *Black Box Thinking*, Matthew Syed, British journalist and table tennis player invites you to think differently about failure.

He refers to the black box that is found in airplanes. When there is a plane crash, the black box is recovered for the purpose of understanding, analyzing, and learning from this failure.

They obtain more information as to what went wrong and why.

They thereby understand how to improve things and prevent the same thing from happening again.

The black box demonstrates that failures and setbacks can be a great source of growth if approached in the right mindset.

Syed refers to the aviation industry, saying that:
'This is a model of an industry where, when there is a failure, it's treated as a very significant learning experience.'
Syed argues that we progress in all kinds of areas by making mistakes.

He was a superb table tennis player, and he knows that every mistake that he made was a learning experience, and at least potentially, a chance to improve.

Why do we not develop this kind of attitude in every sector and every industry? Why not have this attitude in every aspect of our personal and professional life?

Michael Jordan said:

'I've failed over and over and over again in my life and that is why I succeed.'

CRITICAL THINKING: THE PROCESS

There are many ways to map out what critical thinking is all about, and looking up various definitions, it is as follows:

1 -Analyze how parts of a whole interact with each other to produce overall outcomes in complex systems
2 -Make judgments and decisions
3 -Effectively analyze and evaluate evidence, arguments, claims, and beliefs
4 -Analyze and evaluate major alternative points of view
5 -Synthesize and make connections between information and arguments
6 -Interpret information and draw conclusions based on the best analysis
7 -Reflect critically on learning experiences and processes
8 -Solve different kinds of unfamiliar problems in both conventional and innovative ways

CRITICAL THINKING AND CREATIVITY

Many people believe that creativity and critical thinking are complete opposites.

Spoiler alert: They're not!
Think of it, their connection is intimate.

Leading expert and recognized authority on this subject, Dr. Richard Paul stressed the connection between creative thinking and critical thinking.
According to Dr. Paul:
'Sound thinking requires both imagination and intellectual standards.'

When one engages in high-quality thinking, one functions both critically and creatively. One produces, assesses, generates, and judges the products of one's thought.

BEYOND THE AGE OF INFORMATION

Critical thinking also draws on other skills, such as communication and information literacy. **You** need to examine, then analyze, interpret, and evaluate everything.

According to educator Thomas Hoerr, the very notion of intelligence has changed. We no longer rely on the limits of our single mind to access the information resources we need to solve problems.

In today's context, social media, digital connectivity, and advanced technology platforms enable you to enhance your critical thinking skills. **You** engage with other people coming from varied backgrounds and cultures even if on a virtual level.

THE REASON WHY

Drawing on my long experience in the marketing and communication field, one of the early things we learned when discussing brand positioning was 'the reason why'.

We used to ask:
If a brand exists, why is it so? What is it aiming to accomplish?
We almost always asked ourselves this question when faced with a new product.

In their early years, kids ask many questions; in fact, they almost question everything that comes their way, or which they see, or hear. They even challenge you if they are not happy or satisfied with a given response or situation.
They ask you this simple yet powerful question:
'Why?'
You cannot develop your critical thinking without continuously asking this question, 'Why?'

If **you** are not sure of how powerful this is, please take some time and sit with a five-year-old child and have a decent conversation. Asking this simple question is going to prompt you to seek answers and analyze them and debate them with your own self and maybe with others, compelling you to think and see a certain fact from various perspectives.

Now, pause for a moment and think of **'the reason why'.**

Why are you reading this book?
What is it that you wish to accomplish by doing so?

THE EGG AND THE CHICKEN

What came first, the egg or the chicken?

This question is not meant to propel **you** to dive into an endless loop of futile time-wasting. It is not meant to push **you** into a thought process that leads you nowhere, nor is it meant to fuel **you** with raising self-rhetorical and existentialist questions.

On the contrary, it comes as a soft reminder that you will always discover new ways to look at the same issue.

When you think in a critical manner, you look at the same issue beyond the generic answer that we typically see and hear. The binary answer which usually identifies two possible scenarios to a given situation.
An answer that will be either this or that.

But what if the answer can simply be a third entity that has created both the egg and the chicken at once!

COMMUNICATION: HEAR WHAT IS NOT BEING SAID

Now, **you** might be wondering why I chose this to be here and why emotional intelligence is that important?

Before we take a dive into this subject, Daniel Goleman is more like the godfather of this topic and I recommend that you give a fair share of your time to understanding the importance of emotional intelligence.

I will aim to summarize this topic with you in a few sentences, and how Goleman defines it and how it impacts your life at its core, as well as the life of others around you. It really acts like a magic key that can determine both your personal and professional success.

Goleman sets well-defined parameters where he dissects this into the following aspects:

1. Self-Awareness,
2. Self-Management,
3. Relationship Management, and
4. Social Awareness.

You see, once again it all starts with the 'self', with yourself. I will not dwell in the details of the framework above, yet I urge you to do that, as it carries immense benefit if you do so.

The principle thought here that Goleman aimed to lay down is that before reaching out to the world and to others, one must reach a point of being self-aware, and once that is achieved, self-management is as important as the first building block. If these two are managed, then reaching out to others and to the larger social circles becomes a much easier task.

The book *Emotional Intelligence* by Daniel Goleman brings much insight, serving almost as a mental dashboard. Goleman is not just an author, and his credibility is extended further since he is a psychologist and a science journalist as well.

COMMUNICATION IS KEY

Legendary automotive executive Lee Iacocca, known as the godfather of developing the Ford Mustang once said:

'Communication is everything.'

Well, maybe it is not everything, but certainly it is a particularly important skill to develop as a young person and future entrepreneur to be.

Regardless of whatever position and role you are in today, or where you will be in the future, communication is key.
Let me repeat that: Communication is key.

BODY LANGUAGE

There are various types of communication.
The basic types are best identified by the famous work of Albert Mehrabian, who was a Professor Emeritus of Psychology at the University of California, Los Angeles.

He developed a communication model, in which he demonstrated that only 7% of what we communicate consists of the literal content of the message. Seven. Percent.
Where is the remaining 93%?

The use of one's voice, such as tone, intonation, and volume, take up 38%, and as much as 55% of communication consists of body language.

HEAR WHAT IS NOT BEING SAID

My title, 'Hear what is not being said' is inspired from the Mehrabian model. It clearly shows the power and impact of non-verbal communication which constitutes much of the human output.

Effective communication has long been determined as a key foundational skill for any leader.
It is much talked about in the business arena as well as in many fields that require people to communicate together in an effective manner.

You need to know that much of what is not said is already communicated. How you say it is as important as what you say.

The Definitive Book of Body Language by Barbara and Allan Pease, is a good starting point on non-verbal communication.
It acts as an eye opener on this subject.

Most of our communication is not spoken. By understanding body language, **you** develop a better understanding of what is truly being communicated.

By understanding body language, you are already more than halfway there.

WATCH WHAT YOU DON'T SAY

We are often so focused on what others are doing when it comes to non-verbal communication that we forget our own behavior.

The Definitive Book of Body Language is a good reminder. It helps you understand how you read others and equally how they will read you.

For example, did you make sufficient eye contact? Was your handshake firm? What was your posture like? How were you dressed?

All such non-verbal cues make others form a certain perception and opinion of **you**, and vice versa.

CLEAR AND STRAIGHT TO THE POINT

Much literature has been published about the subject of 'communication' and communicating effectively.

Many authors and writers talk about being straight to the point.

I would like to share with you the 7 Cs model.
This model was birthed in the early 1950s in the field of public relations. It was co-created by University of Wisconsin Professor Scott M. Cutlip and Allen H. Center.

The 7 Cs that you will need to communicate are as follows:
Clear, Concise, Concrete, Correct, Coherent, Complete and Courteous.

COMMUNICATION AND COLLABORATION

Again, communication links directly with collaboration, which we have previously covered in the earlier part of this book.

Many behavioral scientists, even in the world of business, speak of communication.

They focus on its relative importance, i.e.:

What is the use of **you** having a great idea and yet you cannot pass it on to others and influence them?

In other words, communication is important for collaboration.

We will see in the chapter on collaboration how groups of people are able to help the individual person.
For now, know that sharp communication – incorporating the 7 Cs – is one of the quickest ways to achieve collaboration.

THE PITCH RECIPE

When pitching critical subjects, one of my mentors gave me a powerful piece of advice.

He said:
'When communicating, always make sure that you have an engaging opening, an interesting middle and a powerful close.'

This became for me like a golden rule that I applied throughout my career. I even use it to this day, and guess what – it works!

Engaging opening.
Interesting middle.
Powerful close.

If you follow this simple recipe, your communication will be so much more powerful and effective as a result.

COMMUNICATION AND TOMORROW

The workspace loves and values communication.
It always did, and it always will.

Expressing thoughts clearly, crisply articulating opinions, communicating coherent instructions, motivating others through powerful speech.

These skills have always been valued in the workplace and in public life.

But in the 21st century, these skills have been transformed and are even more important today. **You** may be asking yourself the question, how has such a key skill of communication been transformed?

Simply put, it is adapted to the current context and environment we live in.

As the **you**th, you must communicate effectively. In order to do so, you need to analyze and process the overwhelming amount of communication in your lives today.

EDUCATION SYSTEM AND COMMUNICATION

While **you** are communicating, there are certain questions **you** need to answer in order to use information to your benefit.

Which information sources are accurate?
Which ones are not?
How can they be leveraged effectively?

The power of modern media and the ubiquity of communication technologies in all aspects of life make teaching strong communication skills even more important.

Education isn't delivering on its goals in communication.
Education emphasizes fluent reading, correct speech, and clear writing.

Evidence shows that students are not mastering even these simple skills at a basic level. I was a lecturer for postgraduate studies in the field of communication.

Each semester I gave students a project that they had to prepare and present. Most of these young students often lagged in at least one of the abovementioned areas.

In the report, 'Are They Really Ready to Work?' employers noted that oral and written communication are among the top four skills they seek in new hires.

Despite this fact, almost all graduates are lacking in these areas. Many employers even noted that employees with degrees were still lacking communication skills.

Read this again: *Employees with degrees were still lacking communication skills.*

DO NOT TAKE COMMUNICATION FOR GRANTED

Communication can be divided into two areas: verbal and non-verbal.

In my previous capacity, as already mentioned, I was a business leader in the communication industry. We hired the best creative talent with excellent communication skills. Despite this fact, they had gaps in one or other areas of their communication.

Again, verbal is one thing and non-verbal is another when it comes to communication.

You will quite often find yourself placed in situations where you would require both areas of communication. These situations require **you** to not just be sufficient at them, but to also be excellent.

At the core of the iNVINCIBLE construct lies communication, and sometimes, one word can change or even save your life. Such is the power of the words we speak. A long time back, we learned the elevator pitch. Imagine that **you** have met the investor of your dreams. Imagine that this person is willing to invest in your idea and you have one minute to communicate it.

Sounds easy? Not at all.

Trust me, even very well-seasoned leaders and communicators still find this a tough call.

Do not take communication for granted. Learning how to communicate effectively is not a walk in the park.

It is said that practice makes perfect. The same with communication – it takes a great deal of practice, and over a prolonged period and in various situations and contexts. Preparedness is probably more than half of the battle in this case.

By preparedness, I mean being both mentally prepared and willing and being up to the task, and also actually rehearsing well all the elements in one single chain all the way from planning to execution. A certain task or event or accomplishment is achieved with a chain of deliverables, including mental, willpower, technical skillset, etc.

You must not expect that you will win at something from having your first go at it though; hence the need for practice and being prepared.

COMMUNICATION TODAY

Brand Watch, a digital consumer intelligence company based in England, carried out a survey and by the end of 2019 the statistics were startling.

To give **you** a glimpse of what goes on across social media platforms, here are some of the findings:

The total worldwide population is 7.8 billion.
The internet has 4.54 billion users.
There are 3.725 billion active social media users.
On average, people have 7.6 social media accounts.
The average daily time spent on social media is 142 minutes per day.
91% of retail brands use two or more social media channels.
81% of all small and medium businesses use some kind of social platform.
Social media users grew by 328 million between October 2018 and October 2019.
That works out at 10 new social media users per second.
Facebook Messenger and WhatsApp handle 60 billion messages per day, and so it goes. Certainly, by the time this book is published these numbers will not be the same and definitely still on the rise.

Communication channels are very, very active.

And the way people communicate today is not like anything in the past.

HUMANS ARE THE CENTER OF NEW TECHNOLOGIES

A similar dynamic applies to the corporate environment.

The workplace is no different.

I recall with my first job in the mid-1990s, we used to communicate by sending letters, and the fax machine was the hero of the day.

Later came email and all the other technology-oriented platforms that helped companies evolve and be more efficient.

The importance of communication has not lessened, despite the different channels through which we now communicate.

There is always a human interaction behind any platform that we use.
In fact, there **will** always be a human interaction behind any platform that we use.

Think about that, and what it implies.

THERE WILL ALWAYS BE A HUMAN INTERACTION BEHIND ANY PLATFORM THAT WE USE.

GLOBALIZATION OF COMMUNICATION

The platforms and channels have changed.
It has become even tougher to communicate effectively and reach your desired audience in such massive clutter.

Additionally, there are now 'global teams' that work together in business. This goes with the principle of working from anywhere, anytime, and reaching anyone.

This is one more reason that people from different cultures, geographies, and linguistic backgrounds are meeting at the same point of communicating together.

The new universal business language is English.
We all know the power of having successful global teams. Companies rely much on having great communication, which in turn contributes directly to the success of any business today regardless of its size.

Today, in times of globalization and the more recent talks of de-globalization and even localization, a young entrepreneur could be anywhere on the planet doing business with people anywhere on earth, not bound by geographical limitations.
The common denominator to all is one word.
That word is 'communication'.

You must master the skill of communicating effectively if you are planning to exist in this new ecosystem and reserve a spot that is relevant to **you.**

MASTER MORE LANGUAGES

The advancement of technology did not kill communication.
On the contrary, it has fueled it.

Today, **you** are compelled to interact with numerous people from various walks of life.

They may exist in different time zones, or countries, or cultures. It is therefore imperative that you learn to communicate clearly and effectively in more than one language.

China and India's populations already constitute almost half of the world's population.

My advice to youth would be to pick up more languages, especially the most commonly spoken languages.
In so doing, it opens up doors to many more people and opportunities.

PICK UP MORE LANGUAGES.
IN SO DOING, IT OPENS UP DOORS TO MANY MORE PEOPLE AND OPPORTUNITIES!

ROBOTS WILL NOT REPLACE HUMANS IN COMMUNICATION

In terms of communication, robots will not replace humans.
Well, not for the next 50 years, at least.

In a recent survey on the future workplace, it was found that one of the top skills that employers look for is having effective communication skills.

True, in some customer relationship jobs we have seen the rise of chatbots and automated AI-assisted software that interact with customers and help them.
This will never replace, at least for the time being, the fact that we are human. Human communication will not fade away anytime soon.

Since the beginning of time, there has been the need to communicate. From the early days of human existence and hunter gathering societies even before spoken language existed, humans felt the need to communicate.

The service economy will always have its fair share in the future.

One of its key facets is communication.

Complex communication involves explanation, negotiation, and other forms of intense human interaction. Jobs that require these skills are not as likely to be automated as others.

For example, you likely use booking.com, Uber, Airbnb, or any other online platform to conduct a certain service. But there is also another element to this equation, and that is the human element.

There may have a robot in the lobby of a hotel assisting you on arrival, but this will never entirely replace the human communication element in the hotel industry – or any industry requiring face-to-face communication for that matter.

NEW WAYS TO DO TRADITIONAL THINGS

The workplace and public life have always valued these skills:

- Expressing thoughts clearly
- Crisply articulating opinions
- Communicating coherent instructions
- Motivating others through powerful speech

In the 21st century, these skills are even more important.
What's more, the ways to achieve them have been transformed.

COMMUNICATE EFFECTIVELY

The communication subject is a vast area.
One can go on to discuss many aspects of it.

To put it in simple terms, communication cannot be effective unless the message is received, and understood, and put in the context in which it is taking place.

Here are some tips for effective communication:

- Communicate clearly
- Articulate thoughts and ideas effectively using oral, written, and non-verbal communication skills in a variety of forms and contexts
- Listen effectively to decipher meaning, including knowledge, values, attitudes, and intentions
- Use communication for a range of purposes (e.g. to inform, instruct, motivate, and persuade)

• Use multiple media and technologies, and know how to assess their impact and effectiveness in relation to your own life a *priori*
• Communicate effectively in diverse environments (including multilingual and multicultural).

CRISIS COMMUNICATION

For example, we have recently gone through the COVID-19 pandemic. Communicating in times of a pandemic or crisis has a completely different approach and way to it. By default, the physical interaction is reduced to its lowest level, hence other forms of communication take place, such as awareness communication and informative communication.

Certainly, the channels have changed, shifting to online presence, hence more awareness is required and more explanation and information sharing would be required to serve this context of a more online approach.

This applies to all of us: personal, professional, even big corporations, and governments.

Public relations firms have an entire specialty and service offering titled 'Crisis communication' which also has its own playbook. Crisis communication focuses on three stages: pre-crisis, during the crisis, and post crisis.
The main role of such communication is 'control and containment', which is done through key messaging that serves such objective.

COMMUNICATION AND COLLABORATION

As already mentioned, communication does not exist in a vacuum.
The moment we raise the topic of communication, it automatically brings us to collaboration. We will dive deeper into collaboration in a standalone chapter to follow.

For now, when we mention communication, we are talking about at least two people or more. Good communication avoids conflict. It persuades.
Good communication is a central skill in negotiation. It resolves disputes, aligns people, and makes for easier agreement on a direction. For everything we wish to accomplish, communication is key.

FOR EVERYTHING WE WISH TO ACCOMPLISH, COMMUNICATION IS KEY!

PERSUASION IS BETTER THAN NEGOTIATION

Dr. William L. Ury, bestselling author of *Getting to Yes and Getting Past No*, showed us how to overcome serious obstacles to negotiation in both of these books.

During my professional career, I attended a training on communication and negotiation. In this workshop, we were assigned different teams, different cases, and different roles.

On one occasion, you took the role of the leader of a group, on another you were a supplier or a service provider, and another time you were an observer.

One week into this workshop, my trainers were still unable to assess my negotiation skills.

This is because, in all the cases that I was given, I managed to communicate well enough and persuade my opponents not to reach conflict.
Without any conflict there is nothing to negotiate on.
Lesson learned:
To start with, why negotiate if you can persuade?

> **WHY NEGOTIATE IF**
> **YOU CAN PERSUADE?**

STORYTELLING

Having spent years in the communication industry, I can tell you one thing with great certainty:
Everyone has a story to share, from individuals to big companies.
The storyteller is a person who tells stories.

Think of it this way: One of your daily tasks is being a storyteller.
People love to hear stories. They want to be inspired. They want to be compelled. People want a story that leaves them with something relevant to their lives, something that they can learn or benefit from.

They also want to add more inspiration to their lives. So, as you begin to integrate this skill into your mix of skills upgrades, just think of yourself as a storyteller. I am certain that when you were young, someone told you a story that left a mark in your mind and imagination.

This could be your mother, your grandfather, or any another person.
Why not be that person yourself?
In other words, why don't you leave a mark on the world's mind?

LEAVE A MARK ON THE WORLD'S MIND!

Whether **you** will be self-employed or in the corporate environment, you will find yourself telling your audiences stories.

Make sure that your stories count. What is meant by this, is to ideally fulfill a meaningful story that will have a positive and sustainable impact to change people's lives for the better.

BE YOUR OWN STORYTELLER AND INSPIRE YOURSELF AND OTHERS. THE WORLD NEEDS YOU!

SPEAK LAST

Nelson Mandela was once asked:
'How do **you** become such a good leader?'

Mandela replied:
'Because I learned to speak last.'

He recalled that as a child he'd accompanied Jongintaba Dalindyebo, the tribal king who raised him, to meetings, which is where he learned this skill.

In our days, we often jump to speak first, but there is much power and growth in training yourself to speak last.

CREATIVITY: IMAGINATION IS MORE IMPORTANT THAN KNOWLEDGE

WHAT CREATIVITY REALLY IS, AND IS NOT!

In many instances, creativity is not understood, and in other instances it is undervalued by society or some intellectual for its lack of definition.

Creativity is not a sporadic whim on a spur of a moment; rather, creative thinking is the process used to generate new, impactful ideas.

The process uses a wide range of idea creation techniques, such as brainstorming, to create new and worthwhile ideas.

New ideas can be classified as both incremental innovations and radical concepts.

Like seeds, we need to nurture new ideas.
This is done through elaborating on initial ideas, which we then refine, analyze, and evaluate to improve and maximize creative efforts.

This requires working creatively with others, being open and responsive to new and diverse perspectives, including understanding the real-world limits to adopting new ideas, and incorporating group input and feedback into the work.

CREATIVITY SEPARATES HUMANS FROM MACHINES

Sir Kenneth Robinson is a leading thinker and speaker on creativity.
He said:
'Creativity is as important in education as literacy, and we should treat it with the same status.'

Unfortunately, in some cultures, creativity gets suppressed and censorship comes as a first reaction to new or novel ideas and events, which may in turn have a detrimental effect on both the future of the **you**th and societies at large.

In today's world of task automation, innovative capacity and a creative spirit are fast becoming requirements for personal and professional success.

CREATIVITY IS WHAT SEPARATES HUMANS FROM MACHINES.

Stressing the importance of creativity, author Daniel Pink remarked:

'The future belongs to a very different kind of person with a very different kind of mind;
creators and empathizers,
pattern recognizers and meaning makers.

These people will now reap society's richest rewards and share its greatest joys.'

CREATIVITY IN A FAST-CHANGING WORLD

If you as the **you**th were to leave school/university without knowing how to continuously create and innovate, you will be underprepared for the challenges of society and the workforce that will come your way in this ever fast-paced changing world.

According to Robert Sternberg of Tufts University:
'Successful individuals are those who have creative skills, to produce a vision for how they intend to make the world a better place for everyone; analytical intellectual skills, to assess their vision and those of others; practical intellectual skills, to carry out their vision and persuade people of its value; and wisdom, to ensure that their vision is not a selfish one.'

Howard Gardner, a reputed American developmental psychologist, cites 'the creating mind' as one of the five minds we'll need in the future.

To cultivate such a mind, he says, we need an education that features 'exploration, challenging problems, and the tolerance, if not active encouragement, of productive mistakes.'

Look up some of his articles published on this subject. You will be amazed to see the power of the mind once harnessed properly!

Creativity is a fundamental aspect of this overall intelligence.

ARTISTIC CREATIVITY

We live in a world in which good design is increasingly used as a means of differentiating objects of mass production. Creative design skills are highly desired in the labor force.

Daniel Pink sums it up best:
'In a world enriched by abundance but disrupted by the automation and outsourcing of white-collar work, everyone must cultivate an artistic sensibility. We may not all be Dali or Degas. But today we must all be designers.'

One of the most talented creators of all time, Pablo Picasso, once said: 'Destruction is the first act of creation.' In other words, if something is to be created, first **you** need to deconstruct what is already there.

DRIVER OF PROGRESS

When it comes to the topic of creativity, some names left their mark on me.

I'd like to bring them to your attention as **you** start attending to this master skill.
They are:
Edward de Bono, Sir Ken Robinson, and Einstein, among others.

Edward de Bono said:
'There is no doubt that creativity is the most important human resource of all. Without creativity, there would be no progress, and we would be forever repeating the same patterns.'

DE BONO

I cannot discuss creativity as a master skill without introducing to you at least a few of the books that really helped me on a practical level during my career and in my life. Edward de Bono is the originator of the term 'Lateral Thinking'.

De Bono has written over 85 books about creativity and subjects related to this topic. Schools from over 20 countries have included de Bono's thinking tools in their curriculum, and he has advised and lectured at board level at many of the world's leading corporations.

When you read de Bono's books, you build a solid foundation for creativity and learn to grow this skill and master it.

At the early stages of my career, I was fortunate that I read more than a dozen of his books, each of which added one building block to the previous one.

Some of his books that could make a difference to you are as follows:

Lateral Thinking, published in 1971 (the year I was born). I read this book in the mid-90s and it was an eye-opener that has helped me think in a more lateral manner – surely this great thinker was way ahead of his time. He introduced this new term and defined it as follows: 'Lateral thinking is a manner of solving problems using an indirect and creative approach via reasoning that is not immediately obvious. It involves ideas that may not be obtainable using only traditional step-by-step logic.'

Six Thinking Hats, published in 1985; and *Serious Creativity: Using the Power of Lateral Thinking to Create New Ideas*, which was published in 1992 and was a summation of many of de Bono's ideas on creativity. *Simplicity* is another great book, as is *How to have creative ideas* published in 2007.

Edward de Bono's book, *Serious Creativity: Using the Power of Lateral Thinking to Create New Ideas* stems from more than 50 years of research on creativity. He shows that creative thinking is vital for business success and that creativity is a skill that you can learn. As summarized by de Bono, here are some of the key takeaways that I believe you need to consider as you engage in creativity.

For starters is de Bono's definition of creativity:
'We all have perceptions, concepts, and boundaries, [and] creativity is about challenging these. Creativity is about breaking patterns and giving us an alternative approach to logical thinking in pursuit of solving problems.
With creativity, we move beyond what is and into what could be.'

He identifies some of the misconceptions on this topic, such as: 'Creativity is something you're born with; it can't be learned'; 'You have to be artistic to be creative'; 'Creativity is crazy and illogical'; etc.

He also clarifies the difference between logical and creative thinking.
He explains that to find the difference, we first need to know a bit about how the brain works. The brain is a self-organizing information system.

That is, it collects and organizes information on the fly. Previous knowledge as well as the order of new information affect how this new information is stored.

Knowing this shows that our concept of 'logical thinking' is fragile.

In logical thinking, we start with a problem and navigate the information we have about that problem until we find a solution. This usually is efficient as we have solved similar problems before, but when there are new problems, we might become stuck in limiting patterns.

Creative thinking helps us break free from these patterns and navigate our knowledge in different ways. In today's world there are many ways to achieve creativity and kick-start the creative process. De Bono refers to a couple of techniques such as 'random input' and 'provocation' that you can use. These techniques assist you to change where you commence the thinking process and therefore end up with other solutions than would have been the case through logical thinking.

The random input and provocation technique both add a new element to what exists, either through challenging the existing or by adding to it, which then leads to a new outcome. This allows you to challenge the current and existing perceptions, concepts and boundaries, and to go beyond them. Knowing that creativity is a master skill that can be taught and learned, it most certainly can be used to your advantage in various contexts and situations in both your personal and professional life.

Referring to the six thinking hats, de Bono explains that there are various hats that you can wear by changing the perspective of how you think, which will in turn help you think better, create better solutions and hence enhance your creative thinking in the way you solve problems, etc.

He described the following: The white hat is about data and information. The red hat is associated with feelings, intuition, and emotion, while the yellow hat is for a positive view of things. He also describes three more hats: the black hat which relates to caution, the green hat for creative thinking and generating new ideas, and the blue hat, which is about process control.

OUT OF THE BOX

Working in the creative industry we always used to hear:
'Out of the box this.'
'Out of the box that.'
'You're stuck in the box.'

The term 'out of the box' means that thinking inside the box is like thinking in a traditional fashion, bound by the old, nonfunctional, or limiting structures, rules, and practices.

Thinking out of the box indicates that great ideas come from outside of the box, not inside it!

GET INVOLVED!

Where do good ideas come from?

In his book, *Where Good Ideas Come From*, Steven Johnson articulates that good ideas don't come from inside someone's head nor from thoughts or visions.

Instead, ideas happen in conversation with colleagues – so if you want a great idea, go to the coffee house and talk to someone!

He builds on the concept of 'adjacent possible' that was created by Stuart Kauffman in 2002. The quote below from Johnson's book explains much of his thinking.

'Go for a walk.
Cultivate hunches.

Write everything down but keep your folders messy. What is meant by that, things don't have to be perfectly aligned and all in place, keep it fluid!

Embrace serendipity

Make generative mistakes
Take on multiple hobbies
Frequent coffeehouses and other liquid networks, where there is some kind of balance between order and chaos.

Follow the links
Let others build on your ideas

Borrow, recycle, re-invent.'
-Steven Johnson

BIOLOGICAL ROOTS OF CREATIVITY

Kauffman is a theoretical biologist who studies the origin of life and the origins of molecular organization.

His concept of ideas proposes that biological systems can morph into more complex systems by making incremental, relatively less energy-consuming changes in their makeup.

Steven Johnson uses this concept to describe how new insights can be generated in previously unexplored areas.

He sums up by saying that good ideas do not come from looking forward or back; rather, they come from looking left and right to what is adjacent to us, and that great innovations are built from the stuff of today, especially things around us that can be combined into something new.

This is 'the adjacent possible' that he refers to.

QUESTIONS TO FIND NEW IDEAS

Johnson suggests that there are seven specific questions that you can ask yourself for finding good ideas:

1 .What new possibilities are there today, that didn't exist a year ago? **(Principle of adjacent possibilities)**
2 .What hunches have you had for some time about what to do? **(Principle of slow hunches** – the more others share them or build on them, the better they may be)
3 .What do fresh eyes think we should do? (**Principle of liquid networks**)
4 .What's worked that's surprised us? (**Principle of serendipity** – build on what surprises, chance happenings)
5 .What's the biggest learning from our biggest error? (**Principle of error**)
6 .What other purpose can our product or service be used for? (**Principle of exaptation** – for example, bird feathers evolved for warmth, and then through 'exaptation' they became wings)
7 .What big success can we build on? (**Platform principle**)

Johnson adds that, 'The patterns are simple, but followed together, they make for a whole that is wiser than the sum of its parts.'

CREATIVITY SETS US APART

Being engaged in brand positioning and marketing services and products, I know that creative thinking and creative design skills are important. They act as the key differentiating factors most of the time.

Early in my career, I was a junior working in the hair and beauty category promoting a shampoo product that we wanted to introduce to the market.

I therefore met with the client seeking a product brief, and we were taught that when introducing new brands and products we need to identify the tangible functional benefits and then map out the emotional benefits that connect with consumers.

When digging for insights, the client said:
'All shampoos come from the same tap. They all have a similar functional benefit. What you need to do is be creative as to what the emotional benefit could be.'

I always recalled this statement throughout my professional career, since he made the point crystal clear that without creative thinking, we all end up generically the same!

CREATIVITY AND TODAY

Various employer surveys have indicated that employers desire talent with creative skills.

In a recent survey carried out by the World Economic Forum, they reviewed labor market trends and identified 10 skills that employees will need in 2020 to thrive in the new technical economy – and creativity was at the top of this list.

Pause for a moment.

Review your skillset and think about your work experience:

Can you think of examples from your work history that demonstrate how you have used creativity skills?

And if you're yet to enter the workforce, how would you imagine your current skillset and your creativity will play out in the real world that you are about to enter?

For perspective, these skills were listed as follows:

Complex problem solving, critical thinking, creativity, people management, coordinating with others, emotional intelligence, judgment, decision-making, service orientation, negotiation, and cognitive flexibility.

SUCCESSFUL ORGANIZATIONS NEED CREATIVE MINDS

Howard Gardner is an American developmental psychologist known for his theory of 'multiple intelligences' and his book, *Five Minds of the Future* cites that 'the creating mind' is one of the five minds we'll need in the future.

To cultivate such a mind, he says, we need an education that features 'exploration, challenging problems, and the tolerance, if not active encouragement, of productive mistakes.' Gardner writes in his book that, 'if creativity does not infiltrate the DNA of an organization, it is unlikely to be passed on to the next generation.'

According to him, successful organizations need to 'fill their leadership team with individuals who are proven creators' and that this leadership team needs to work closely with 'early adapters and ingenuous users', tapping their ideas and giving plenty slack to those who think out of the box.

However, he also warns that, 'at a deep level . . . creativity is a chancy undertaking that can never be guaranteed – only fostered or thwarted.'

Gardner refers to creativity as a blessing and maybe a curse.
He gives the example that throughout history there were creative minds, but they were not appreciated at all.

On the contrary, the system rejected them at first!
Galileo Galilei comes to mind, but at least he wasn't burnt at the stake and merely had to officially recant his ideas.

People such as Bach and Vincent van Gogh, Freud and Darwin were not appreciated at first.

Although creative individuals are all too often discouraged or ignored by those in power, Seely Brown is right when he says: 'to thrive in the future, organizations and individuals will have to be creative or be left behind.'

SCHOOL IS NOT ENOUGH

To put this in today's context, let's consider the massive changes and the fast pace of a changing world, due to the pandemic. Many sectors and organizations have gone out of business and others are struggling to maintain their existence.

Many of these businesses have surely paid the price for not having encouraged creativity as a key pillar in their corporate culture and narrative, hence falling short of being creative about how they approach issues and problems. In the past, we have witnessed many examples of this, such as the downfall of Nokia and Kodak, among others.

My advice for you, the youth of today is not to solely rely on your schools, universities or companies to nurture your creative skills.

Instead, you need to jump on the wagon and seek other sources.
Sources that are more relevant, and which can help you develop this skill by challenging your own mind, heart, and gut. Sources such as the books and authors I have quoted within these pages.

GIVE CREATIVITY ITS OWN RIGHT

Beyond the creative agencies that I worked in which measured creativity, recognized it and rewarded it as part of the employee evaluation, I can't think of many good examples that really stand out!

To a large extent, current systems, be it corporate, educational, or societal, push for conformity, consistency, and compliance.

We have seen roles in the creative agency business such as chief creative officer. My question today is: What other companies have this role? Or, even further than this, what about a chief inspiration officer, chief innovation officer, etc.?

We, on a global scale are lagging behind when it comes to creativity and little is being utilized when it comes to human intelligence and capacity of the creative mind. For creativity to be nurtured, much responsibility lies on the shoulders of the education system and governmental policies at large. This same responsibility extends to companies and corporations, however, it is ultimately the responsibility of each individual person who is willing to develop this skill. In other words, the creativity ball is in your court.

> **WE NEED TO RECOGNIZE THE VALUE CREATIVITY BRINGS TO AN ORGANIZATION AND REWARD IT ACCORDINGLY.**

WHAT HINDERS CREATIVITY?

Many managers, especially those who are less secure about themselves, have a hard time working with people who push boundaries and challenge the way things are done.

They don't want to be challenged.
They don't want the bar raised.
They don't want to explain why something needs to stay the same.
All of this is exhausting to them.

It's much easier to just ignore, dismiss, or add layers of management to dilute the impact these people can have.

The problem with this approach is that you dilute what your organization is capable of. Embracing people who think differently is not a sign of weakness as a leader. Rather, it is a strength, especially if used for the betterment of the organization.
Notice: I'm not advocating for embracing everyone who thinks differently.

EMBRACING PEOPLE WHO THINK DIFFERENTLY CAN BRING INCALCULABLE ADDED VALUE.

This area might pose a challenge for you as the youth, as you graduate and enter the workforce and must find ways to work with your direct line managers. However, the essence of it is finding a common, healthy breathing space to maintain the creative output.

YOU ARE NOT BORN AN INNOVATOR

This brings me to Sir Ken Robinson, who explicitly spoke of this in his book, *Finding Your Element*, and spread this message as to how you can discover your talent and passions and transform your life.

He did many speeches on this in TEDx and other platforms.

He shared valuable messages, among which is that college is not everything. Instead, you really need to find your own vibe and sing your own song.

Again, creativity does not exist in a vacuum.
You are not born an innovator.
Innovation is closely intertwined with some of the other skills previously identified.

Innovation today has a social component. It requires adaptability, leadership, teamwork, and interpersonal skills.

Today more than ever, the capacity to innovate is linked to the ability to connect with others, and with a facility for communication and collaboration and ways to integrate creativity.

HERE'S TO THE CRAZY ONES

Steve Jobs wrote the famous brand manifesto for Apple in 1997:
'Here's to the crazy ones.'

'Here's to the crazy ones,
the misfits, the rebels, the troublemakers, the round pegs in the square holes,
the ones who see things differently.

They're not fond of rules...
You can quote them, disagree with them, glorify or vilify them.
About the only thing you can't do is ignore them, because they change things – they push the human race forward.
And while some may see them as the crazy ones, we see genius.

MY TWO CENTS

To me, creativity is like something new being born, just like a newborn baby when two people get together in the act of love and co-create a third entity, a new soul, a new talent, a new person who carries the seed and DNA of the previous two.

If knowledge is power, then creativity is superpower.

Because the ones who are crazy enough to think that they can change the world, are the ones who do.'

COLLABORATION: LONELY WOLVES DIE HARD

COMPOUNDED FORCE

When I was young in my twenties, I always thought I could do things on my own.

As we navigate through life, we learn various lessons. One of those big lessons for me was learning the true value of collaboration.

When different minds are put together, they form a compounded force, assuming that these minds are travelling in the same direction.

Collaboration brings richness to any given problem, issue or idea.
Different people bring with them different points of views, and hence their cumulative experiences as well.

Many international researchers have demonstrated that a major component of character building is collaboration.
We often think that when we collaborate we lose part of ourselves.
In reality, we gain new parts of ourselves that we didn't know or possess before.

> **WHEN WE COLLABORATE, WE GAIN NEW PARTS OF OURSELVES THAT WE DIDN'T KNOW OR POSSESS BEFORE.**

COLLABORATION: SURVIVAL MECHANISM

There are many things to be learned from the animal kingdom. After all, we are social animals in some way and form.

In their book, *A Cooperative Species*, Samuel Bowles and Herbert Gintis, pioneers in the new experimental and evolutionary science of human behavior, show that the central issue is not why selfish people act generously, but instead how genetic and cultural evolution have produced a species in which substantial numbers make sacrifices to uphold ethical norms and to help even total strangers.

They demonstrate that collaboration and cooperation among humans is as vital as it is necessary.

The authors describe how, for thousands of generations, cooperation with fellow group members has been essential to survival.

Groups that created institutions to protect the civic-minded from exploitation by the selfish flourished and prevailed in conflicts with less cooperative groups.

Key to this process was the evolution of social emotions such as shame and guilt, and our capacity to internalize social norms so that acting ethically became a personal goal, rather than simply a prudent way to avoid punishment.

COOPERATION IS WITH NATURE

Why do humans, uniquely among animals, cooperate in large numbers to advance projects for the common good?

One cannot discuss the subject of collaboration without referring to Charles Darwin's thinking on this topic, as he addressed it in both *The Descent of Man* and *On the Origin of Species*.

For Darwin, sexual selection was crucial to understanding why human society operated the way it did. The relationships between the sexes, which for Darwin were both cooperative and competitive, symbolized perfectly the tension between cooperation and competition at the heart of modern life. When we think of cooperation, and plugging it in the context of today's world, 'competition' pops up to the surface, as we live in a highly competitive world, especially the business world.

In *The Descent of Man*, Darwin stresses that cooperation isn't contrary to nature. As opposed to the idea that some people have, that natural selection selects purely for selfish qualities, Darwin was quite clear that natural selection can select for cooperative and collaborative qualities.
He also pointed out that the process of selection for cooperative and collaborative qualities is not a serene parade of agreeableness – rather, it's the result of often violent conflicts.

It's because we live in a world which frequently experiences such conflicts that our collaborative qualities are so important.

In his book, *The Origins of Virtue*, Matt Ridley argues that cooperation and virtue are just as deep-rooted in human nature as selfishness.

He restated the message which was already there in *The Descent of Man*, but which had somehow been forgotten. What this book did was popularize the idea that cooperation can indeed be favored by natural selection.

Paul Seabright, a respected professor in economics and the author of many books, also addressed the subject of cooperation in a couple of his books, *The Company of Strangers* and *The War of the Sexes*.
He put forward the idea that the capacity of humans to cooperate is extraordinary. He said that cooperation is in some sense a natural ability that we have and to cooperate is part of nature.

He stresses the point that coming from the world of economics, many assumptions were made to portray selfishness and competition as natural traits instead of cooperation. He believes the opposite! He also believes that collaboration should not be portrayed as an artificial construct to human nature.

In his words: 'I first wanted to show that cooperation was a natural talent and therefore something we could learn about by looking at how our natural talents have evolved. But secondly, to emphasize that it's a natural talent that's being exercised in a very different setting from the way it used to be exercised.'

COLLABORATION VS. COOPERATION

When discussing collaborative leadership, Jesse Lyn Stoner made the point clear that collaboration is one thing and cooperation is another.
She is a business consultant, coach, and former executive. She made this point along with her bestselling coauthor, Ken Blanchard, in their international bestseller, *Full Steam Ahead: Unleash the Power of Vision.*

Quite often these terms, collaboration and cooperation, are used and interchanged when they do not really mean the same thing. She provides the following definition to both, making the key distinction that collaboration happens under a shared vision while cooperation does not. She defines each of them as follows:

'***Collaboration*** is working together to create something new in support of a shared vision. The key points are that it is not through individual effort, something new is created, and that the glue is the shared vision.'

'***Cooperation*** is important in networks where individuals exchange relevant information and resources in support of each other's goals, rather than a shared goal. Something new may be achieved as a result, but it arises from the individual, not from a collective team effort. Cooperation can be defined simply as the action or process of working together to the same end.'

21ST CENTURY: COLLABORATION BEYOND PHYSICAL CONFINES

Collaboration has become a common term in today's world.

Moving through the 21st century, although we might be digitally connected and working from home or from any environment that is not of corporate nature, especially for freelancers, you would still find yourself in multiple scenarios and situations where you must collaborate to reach a certain goal, objective, or result.

Collaboration is not necessarily defined by a confined physical space, although some business leaders believe it is of high importance for staff and employees to be physically under one roof maintaining physical and face-to-face contact.

CULTURE OF COLLABORATION

For example, Jesse Lyn Stoner refers to Marissa Mayer's decision back in 2013 to bring Yahoo employees back to the office under the idea that it would be important to enhance collaboration when working side by side.

Stoner observes that such a decision might have created better teamwork, cooperation, communication and coordination, but not necessarily building and creating collaboration, since for collaboration to work, there should be a 'culture' that supports it.

True, collaboration usually takes place within a certain context, the underlying foundation of which, is the word 'culture'.
For example, the kind of values a certain company has, will dictate the way it conducts itself.

These values dictate how it operates and how it achieves results and how it rewards performance, etc.

OPEN-SOURCE PROJECTS

The importance of collaboration sites such as Wikipedia highlight how interconnected our world has become and emphasizes the benefits of collaborative work.

The resulting products are those to which millions of users have contributed. The comprehensive nature of the articles on Wikipedia reflects the collaborative culture of the site and demonstrates how people working together can produce extremely inclusive and valuable resources.

Python is another great example. Python is a programming language with more than 10 million users worldwide and is maintained by an elite of minds across the globe who have this same shared interest.This is a perfect concrete area where collaboration is put to action at its best.

DRIVING IMPACT

Generally, collaboration has been accepted as a skill that's essential to achieve meaningful and effective results. However, in the past decade it has become increasingly clear that collaboration is not only important but also necessary for students and employees, due to globalization and the rise of technology.

Another great example is The Global Learning and Observations to Benefit the Environment (GLOBE) Program. It is a worldwide, hands-on, primary and secondary school-based science and education program, that illustrates how students are collaborating with each other to impact global problems. GLOBE's vision promotes and supports students, teachers, and scientists to collaborate on inquiry-based investigations of the environment and the Earth system working in close partnership with NASA, the National Oceanic and Atmospheric Association (NOAA), and the National Science Foundation's (NSF) Earth System Science Projects (ESSPs) in studying and researching the dynamics of Earth's environment.

Over 1.5 million students have participated in GLOBE, contributing more than 21 million measurements to the GLOBE database for use in their inquiry-based science projects. More projects like GLOBE are needed for students to be prepared for a global, technology-based workforce.

WISDOM OF THE CROWDS

Various scholars and authors have emphasized the importance of collaboration.

Author James Surowiecki, for example, explains how we use the 'wisdom of crowds' in the new economy by saying that 'under the right circumstances, groups are remarkably intelligent, and are often smarter than the smartest people in them.' Wisdom of the crowd is used in many social studies.

I urge you to refer to the 'Wisdom of Crowds' study carried out by Stanford University. It answers many of the questions that fall in this subject area. One of the more recent trends that we have been witnessing, for example, is 'crowdsourcing'.

Surowiecki underscores the importance of collaboration by remarking that '... a large group of diverse individuals will come up with better and more robust forecasts and make more intelligent decisions than even the most skilled "decision-maker."'

Diversity brings multiple individual and cultural perspectives into the collaboration. Not only does a collaborative effort create more holistic results than individual efforts, but it also creates knowledge for a greater number of people.

As a result, if you as an individual are wired to working collaboratively, and come across other individuals who feel the same, then the group can generate more knowledge, making collaboration a key ingredient to your own success and the success of the entire group. This is a much-needed skill to harness in today's global society.

COLLABORATION WITH THE UNIVERSE

Collaboration with the universe (self & others) can go a long way. Here I wish to bring your attention to the book titled, *You are the Universe: Discovering Your Cosmic Self and Why it Matters.*

This is more of an art piece that was written by Deepak Chopra (whom I was fortunate to meet in 2007 in Chicago) who joined forces with leading physicist Menas Kafatos.

If you read this book, you will get to explore some of the most important questions about your place in the world.

In essence, *You Are the Universe* means just that: you are a co-creator of what we call reality, and this extends even to the limits of time and space. Think about that, and the implications it holds for you.

WE ALL INHERIT CERTAIN PREDEFINED REALITIES: IT IS ALL UP TO YOU WHETHER YOU EMBRACE WHAT IS OR CHOOSE TO CHANGE IT.

EMOTIONAL INTELLIGENCE: IT'S ALL ABOUT EQ

Emotional intelligence is key when it comes to collaboration.
We need emotional intelligence for effective communication. Effective communication leads to better collaboration.

In my view, IQ took center stage for many years, and it was believed to be the hero of the day. This was true until more studies were conducted on EQ. The best summation of IQ and EQ can be put in this short sentence:

'EQ eats IQ for breakfast.'

'EQ EATS IQ FOR BREAKFAST.'

CONNECTENESS: REACH OUT

YOU ARE THE AVERAGE OF THE FIVE PEOPLE YOU SPEND TIME WITH

I am certain that you are very familiar with this: 'You are the average of the five people you spend the most time with,' a quote attributed most often to motivational speaker Jim Rohn.

Factoring this in mind, you need to audit the people around you.

Make sure that you're spending time with people who are in line with what you want for your own life – and preferably people 'better' than you, so it raises your average.

I urge you to pause for a minute and do this simple exercise of actually writing down the names of the five people you spend most of your time with. You may be surprised with your own answer, which as a first-hand observation alone can be so compelling that you start making immediate changes to your life.

START SMALL

According to anthropologist Robin Dunbar, humans have a natural limit to the number of meaningful relationships they can have.
This number is about 150.

In recent years, Dunbar has taken his idea further by considering the emotional closeness between individuals.

This is referred to as Dunbar's number. Dunbar studied this subject on primates and, looking at the size of the human brain, made this extrapolation to conclude that humans can maintain around 150 meaningful relationships.

That said, it is not the number that counts here. Rather, what is important is connecting with others who you are able to maintain meaningful and healthy relationships with. This in turn will have a direct and positive impact on your life.

POSITIVE RELATIONSHIPS HAVE A POSITIVE IMPACT ON YOUR LIFE.

TWO-PIZZA TEAMS

Dunbar's number has become of interest in anthropology, evolutionary psychology, and business management. Developers of social networks, and even modern military formations have utilized such thinking when it comes to creating policies related to maintaining or improving unit cohesion and morale.

Similar literature and evidence were found in other social studies, which reflected how hunter gatherer societies behaved, from the formations of the Roman legions to the modern-day effective businesses.

Jeff Bezos, who spoke about the two-pizza rule, refers to it as the secret of Amazon's success. In the early days of Amazon, Jeff Bezos instituted a rule:

'Every internal team should be small enough that it can be fed with two pizzas.'

CONNECTING THE WORLD, BUT...

Reaching out to people is key.
So is nurturing these relationships.

The rise of social media platforms has made connectedness easier in many ways.

The question you need to ask though, is this:
Who do I connect with, and why?

We are not talking about fake or superficial connections. We are looking at the importance of you being connected and being part of one or two or more networks, ecosystems, etc.

THE MASTERMIND GROUP

A key skill which I share with my clients is learning to form their mastermind group.

What is it all about? And how does forming a mastermind group sit at the heart of connectedness?

It is through being able to be more effective and more powerful by leveraging this connectedness with others and tapping into their knowledge and resources.

In my capacity as a certified business coach, we learned through the coaching program that there are various sources of knowledge available to you beyond what you already know and have learned on a personal and individual manner.

In his book *Think and Grow Rich*, Napoleon Hill defines that a mastermind is the coordination of knowledge and effort in a spirit of harmony, between two or more people, for the attainment of a definite purpose. Hill explains that the mastermind has two characteristics: one is economic in nature, and the other is psychic.

He explains that forming your own mastermind group is the basis of good fortune. When people of good energy meet, they create a larger field of play that taps into the infinite and abundant intelligence.

He provides multiple examples from history of big names who made a huge success of their lives. The common thing between them: they had a mastermind group.

Important to note here is that your group is not limited to a specific number of people; it can be 5 or 20 or even 100, if it serves the principle of shared economic interest and the same energy field of play. More so, in our world today, such formation of a mastermind group is not limited to a physical meeting place, but rather can happen virtually in every sense of the word. It has become a more fluid space for like-minded people to gather.

WE LEARN FROM EACH OTHER

Upon studying the key components of entrepreneurship, connectedness pops up as one of the critical success factors for future entrepreneurs.

Henry Sebata, an entrepreneur himself, said that having a network of useful people who can help you think is extremely crucial.

Entrepreneurs learn more from each other than most people can imagine. If you consider yourself as an entrepreneur, why not bounce ideas off the people you have gathered in your network?

Every angle adds to your overall view.
Every opinion adds to your overall narrative.

This expanded view and narrative will in turn enhance your decisions.

EVERY ANGLE ADDS TO YOUR OVERALL VIEW. EVERY OPINION ADDS TO YOUR OVERALL NARRATIVE.

HOW DOES YOUR FRIEND'S FRIEND'S FRIEND FEEL?

When observing the science of social networks, you are certainly influenced by the people around you. This type of influence does not stop anywhere near the five people you spend the most time with. It is far more dispersed. Research carried out by Christakis and Fowler proved that you are influenced by people whom you have not even met, who fall in the category of friends of friends.

The most telling study results were about happiness.

The two researchers found that happy friends make you happier, which is expected, but if your friend of a friend of a friend is happy with their life, then you have a six percent greater likelihood of being happy yourself.

What is six percent? It might not seem like much, but consider that other studies suggest that if I gave you a $10,000 raise, that would only trigger about a two percent increase in your happiness.

MY TWO CENTS

Your friends are your future. Really!

The implication here is that you don't just need to be more deliberate about who you're spending the most time with. Rather, you need to be examining your entire network and its influence on your life.
Who are you spending your time with?

In summary, yes, it may start with the average of the five people you surround yourself with, but it is way bigger than that. You are the average of all the people who surround you. So, take a moment to pause, look around you and make sure you're in the right company.

RESILIENCE: BE READY TO BOUNCE BACK

THIS IS HOW WINNING IS DONE

In 2020, I published an article about resilience titled: 'Building Resilience, Lessons Learned from My Grandfather.'

I took him as an example of what resilience is all about.

As I wrote this article, various definitions and meanings popped up as to what the best way to define this word is.

An image kept coming to my mind.
It was from the movie Rocky Balboa, when Rocky said to his son:
'It ain't about how hard you hit, it's about how hard you can get hit and keep moving forward. This is how winning is done.'

As the years pass by, I reflect on those words.

This quote is simple.
It explains what resilience is all about.
In essence, resilience is just like any muscle. You attend to it. You exercise it. It grows.

RESILIENCE IS LIKE A MUSCLE

Resilience is the ability to deal with high levels of
challenge while minimizing negative outcomes; staying or getting back on track to achieve your goals and growing stronger.

You have the foundations of resilience within you.
Resilience is just like a muscle that you engage when you encounter difficult situations.

You can strengthen this muscle through practice on both the mental and physical levels.

'When we learn how to become resilient, we learn how to embrace the beautifully broad spectrum of the human experience' Jaeda Dewalt wrote.

JEDDO NAJIB: A SERIES OF UNFORTUNATE EVENTS

I was fortunate enough to have spent my childhood years with my late grandfather, where in his form of daily storytelling much of his personal stories provided ample wisdom. One of which is the story of resilience.
My grandfather witnessed a series of unfortunate events.

Here is the timeline of these events:
He was born in Mount Lebanon in 1904 and by the time he was 10 years old, World War One (1914–1918) was at his doorstep. The chronology of events took a deep dive thereafter, when in 1915–1916 a large locust swarm invaded their agricultural society followed by a severe famine that lasted for three years (1915–1918). Next, they were hit with the Spanish flu pandemic (1918–1919) and the cherry on top was the end of the Turkish rule and the French mandate in 1923. For perspective and to the young readers, Mount Lebanon, my grandfather's birthplace went through two different foreign mandates of occupation by foreign powers, the Turks and the French, hence it was not the best of times for the local inhabitants of that land, where many sanctions and restrictions were imposed impacting their day-to-day lives, stability, and basic needs.
Many people perished, migrated, or even mentally gave up!
It was a time to survive and not thrive!

They had neither technology nor master's degrees from the Ivy League nor startup funding from Silicon Valley, and they were geographically bound to where they lived.

Looking back at this story, it was told with much passion and the key lesson that emerges out of it is one word:

Resilience.

JEDDO NAJIB: BEHAVIORAL TRAITS

Jeddo Najib learned about farming the land, started an apprenticeship as a stonemason, and traded livestock all at once.

He juggled many balls at the same time just like a magician in a circus.

He also carried and built certain behavioral traits within him to pass through this period of almost a decade of events, some of which can be characterized as follows:

1. Being positive and confident.
2. He knew his priorities and was creative about trying new things.
3. He had a good connection with his environment and collaborated to help others and in return was helped.
4. He had some level of good planning and structure to consistently do what he did.

WHAT TO LEARN FROM MY GRANDFATHER NAJIB

What can individuals and corporations learn from this?
There is no better time than now for understanding resilience and developing it within yourself.
We are living in times of witnessing the convergence of three different potent cycles at once:

1. Pandemic
2. Economic
3. Cognitive

We all interact and deal at the core of these cycles and one way or another we are greatly impacted both individually as well as collectively by what happens in these cycles.

Such potency can throw you off your path or the norms of what you knew or what you did to survive and thrive.
They can knock you down, on many fronts, from the physical to the mental state of your being.

Building resilience applies to corporations of the future as much as it applies to individuals.
There may be variations between the individual and the corporation, yet brands and corporations are made of people and behave to a large extent with similar motivations to individuals.

Building resilience allows both individuals and corporations to deal with difficult situations more skillfully and prove the ability to cope with changes at home, at work, and in
society. For individuals it increases strength, and for corporations, it allows them to design strategies to build a robust system and structure and generate effective approaches to shared challenges.

In a nutshell: Resilience is a powerful muscle, and you need to exercise it well.

RESILIENCE IS A POWERFUL MUSCLE. EXERCISE IT WELL!

PART TWO - YOU AND THE FAST-CHANGING WORLD

YOU AND THE NEW ECOSYSTEM

The new ecosystem of today is no longer a case of yes or no, black or white. Here, one key word strikes my mind, and that is: Maybe.

The 'maybe' state of being is best envisaged and recited in 'The Story of the Chinese Farmer' narrated by Alan Watts and it goes like this:

*Once upon a time there was a Chinese farmer whose horse ran away. That evening, all of his neighbors came around to commiserate. They said, 'We are so sorry to hear your horse has run away. This is most unfortunate.' The farmer said, '**Maybe**.' The next day the horse came back bringing seven wild horses with it, and in the evening everybody came back and said, 'Oh, isn't that lucky. What a great turn of events. You now have eight horses!' The farmer again said, '**Maybe**.'*

*The following day his son tried to break one of the horses, and while riding it, he was thrown and broke his leg. The neighbors then said, 'Oh dear, that's too bad,' and the farmer responded, '**Maybe**.' The next day the conscription officers came around to conscript people into the army, and they rejected his son because he had a broken leg. Again all the neighbors came around and said, 'Isn't that great!' Again, he said, '**Maybe**.'*

The whole process of nature is an integrated process of immense complexity, and it's really impossible to tell whether anything that happens in it is good or bad because you never know what will be the consequence of the misfortune; or, you never know what will be the consequences of good fortune.

— Alan Watts

Often, we label our experience as 'bad' if we hate it, and 'good' if we like it. But the bad cannot exist without the good, and vice versa.
Whatever happens in our life, we'll never know the consequences it may bring in the future. As Alan Watts said: 'You never know what will be the consequence of the misfortune; or, you never know what will be the consequences of good fortune.'

LIKE NOTHING WE KNEW

As you start preparing yourself, building and sharpening the soft skills discussed in Part One, you will now be ready to plug yourself in the new world.

For this though, you need to have a good understanding of the new reality by asking yourself the question:

What does this new world look like?

This new world is not like anything we knew in the past.
This new world is fast evolving.

THIS NEW WORLD IS NOT LIKE ANYTHING WE KNEW IN THE PAST.
THIS NEW WORLD IS FAST EVOLVING.

YOU ARE IN THE DRIVER'S SEAT

Before you plug yourself in this new world, you really need to make sense of the new reality that we are seeing today, and find yourself a spot in it that is relevant to you and this new ecosystem.

If you are unable to do this, you will most likely become irrelevant and will be left behind.

Important to note here is that you are in the driver's seat.
You will not receive a straight answer from your parents with regard to the future, as they represent the generation before you. Most of the pieces of advice that they will give you will be based on what they knew and lived before and the knowledge that it brings.

You will not get a straight answer from the schooling system, either. It is outdated to a large extent and still functions in an old-fashioned mode.

In college today, you are programmed to study a certain major or to specialize in a certain subject such as engineering, medicine, etc. However, in my opinion, you are much better off studying the people and companies that not only change the world, but literally change the way you live today and thrive in tomorrow's reality.

BEYOND COVID-19

One cannot ignore but must instead observe companies like Amazon, Facebook, Google, Tesla, Apple, Uber, etc., and this list is growing all the time.

Writing this book coincided with the COVID-19 pandemic and also with a few other incidents that are as significant and taking place, but perhaps in a more silent manner.

A good example would be the social media share of space and its impact which will be felt for decades to come. Another example is China's announcement of launching its mission to Mars to build a permanent station there.

True quantum computing may not be making headlines yet, but rest assured that its impact will be substantial at the heart of your life and many areas that impact you directly. In late 2019, Google took a quantum leap in computer science by solving a problem that had been regarded as almost impossible for normal computers. By using its quantum computer, named Sycamore, the organization has claimed 'quantum supremacy' over the most powerful supercomputers in the world. This is a game-changer, and the effects will be huge.

THE FOURTH WAVE

Michio Kaku, the renowned scientist and quantum physicist gave a great speech in 2018 titled *Michio Kaku's Ten Predictions for the Future,* and he asked one major key question:
'What is the fourth wave of wealth generation?'

He goes on to say that science and technology come in waves, and we are due for our next wave which he calls the fourth wave.

In his view, the first wave was the discovery of steam power which took place in the 1800s.
Eighty years later came the electric age.
Another 80 years later came the computer.

Now, we are talking about science at the molecular level.
According to him, the fourth wave will be all about Artificial Intelligence, Nanotechnology, and Biotechnology.

He considers them to be the drivers of wealth generation as we step into the future.

YOUR TWENTIES: EXPLORE!

After giving a long list of examples of how the world is changing and will change almost on every level, Michio Kaku simply says: 'We are talking about a world where if you can imagine it, you can create it.'

It may sound a bit romantic, but it is as real as can be.

In your teens you are literally like a sponge, but in your twenties it is time to explore – yes, to explore beyond your boundaries and, by exploration, I mean step out of your limitations that are set by your own self and others, and explore new experiences, passions, travel, and learning about other cultures. One day soon you will realize that your growth is a cumulative non-linear multiple of experiences that add up to who you are today.
In the process, nothing is truly lost, it simply transforms.

YOUR THIRTIES: DO WHAT YOU LOVE

Once you step into your thirties, you have cumulated more knowledge, more exposure, and more grit to go about things. Being self-fulfilled can only be determined and defined by you and only you.

It's all in the name, 'You are the system', meaning that you create your own reality. Earlier in the book I also mentioned that success is relative.

It is a great place to be doing what you love and loving what you do.
The material reward, if you are after it, will eventually find its way to you in the process.

There will always be someone interested in what you do.
There will always be someone interested in what you have to say.
There will always be someone interested in what you love and contribute to this world.

> **THERE WILL ALWAYS BE SOMEONE INTERESTED IN WHAT YOU LOVE.**

WORLD ON FAST-FORWARD

The headlines you read today are so different from what you read just ten years ago, and even what you will read in less than only two years from now. The world is on fast-forward!

Today you see topics that are occupying the planet.
You read about climate change.
You read about megacities.
You read about the demographic explosion. The world population is nearing eight billion!

When did you ever imagine reading an article discussing 'Space economy and space travel', or even saying 'Let's zoom', which became a new verb in our vocabulary overnight!

THREAT OR OPPORTUNITY?

This can only tell us that the only constant is change.

It is and will always be your choice whether you see this as either an opportunity or a threat.

It is up to you what side of the fence you choose to be.

IT IS UP TO YOU WHAT SIDE OF THE FENCE YOU CHOOSE TO BE.

If I mention traffic jams to you, would your mind see it as a burden, or as an opportunity to create a solution about it?
Uber saw it as an opportunity.

If I speak to you about housing and lodging, would you see it as an obstacle, or would you challenge yourself to find a more convenient way to go about it? Airbnb chose the latter.

And what about lockdowns in times of pandemics, when you cannot communicate as effectively?
Would you think of it as an issue, or would you find a way around it?

Zoom found a way around it.

The list of examples goes on.

NEW REALITY

This new world order is allowing scalability of anything you wish to do beyond boundary and limit.

Would you see robots as a threat to your work, or will you create an attitude to work alongside them?
Choose your perspective.

To put this fast-paced change in a more concrete form, a study was published by Korn Ferry Global in 2021 titled 'Making change happen'.

The study shed some light on how the near future will appear and its impact across individuals, talent, companies, and the workplace.

According to this study, by 2030, nearly 9% of the world's population will live in just 41 megacities.
By 2029, it is predicted that robots will have reached the same intelligence as humans. Thirty-five percent of the skills considered important today, won't be in five years' time.
More startling is that 65% of children entering primary school today, will perform jobs that we have never even heard of.

Take a minute.
Reflect on this new reality.
Bring it back to you.

Do this, and develop your own mindset and skillset, with which to navigate the new world ahead of you.

CHANGE IS HAPPENING

What we know and are witnessing already is that after COVID-19, the workplace has changed.

According to the Korn Ferry survey of 1,000 companies, companies are operating more virtually almost at a 75% rate, 47% are communicating with their workforces in a different way, 36% have deployed less contingent labor, and most importantly is that 27% of these companies are retraining and reskilling their employees because the needs are changing in this new order.

So what do these numbers really mean? It means that things as we knew them have already changed, including social behaviors and the way we conduct our work, interact with others, what we knew, as well as our skills. It literally means that the way we conduct our lives has changed!

THE GREAT RESET. TECHNOLOGY AND BEYOND

THE FUTURE IS HERE

The writing is on the wall: We are witnessing the Great Reset.

We are truly witnessing a crossing between the past and the future.

The future is here now, your future, and so is the collective's.

Peter Diamandis, in his book titled *The Future is Faster Than You Think,* delves into a host of converging technologies and how they will disrupt businesses, industries, and our lives in the decades ahead.

He stresses the fact that today's emerging technologies are already building upon (and accelerating) each other's growth. Whether in transportation, retail, advertising, education, health, entertainment, food, or finance, their convergence will have a profound – and irreversible – impact on every aspect of our lives.

Your future lies in your own hands once you can understand this ever-changing landscape and the Great Reset we are living as we speak.

Without a doubt, it is enabled by technology.

In the language of astrology and cosmology, this period that we are stepping into is described as the Age of Aquarius. You don't have to be a strict believer in the mentioned areas of science, but you may wish to be curious enough to delve a bit in both and aim to deduct and relate how this Age of Aquarius relates to our current reality and everyday life.

We are leaving behind the power struggles, money, and control, and stepping more into a new age that is best represented by collaboration, humanitarianism, and peace.

Now, regardless of the above description, we do know that there are already many predictions and signs that tell us that we are stepping into a new world order, or, to make it more concrete, that our world as we knew it has changed.

KEY PREDICTIONS FOR 2030

The World Economic Forum's agenda captured some of the key predictions that will take place in the coming decade reaching to 2030. Some of these predictions highlight the following:

1. All products will become services.
2. A global price on carbon.
3. A handful of global players beyond the single dominance of the USA.
4. The healthcare system is disrupted, hence they title it as 'Farewell hospital, hello home-spital'.
5. Food habits will change, from eating less meat to eating more healthily, and to a convenient and redesigned way of living.
6. More and more displaced people, estimated around 1 billion globally, hence they provide the example of how today's refugees might be the CEOs of tomorrow.
7. The testing of the Western democracies and the rise of new systems and values.
8. And within no time, people will be starting to relocate to the red planet.

INNOVATIONS ACROSS SECTORS

In another study titled 'Future shocks – and how technology could change the world in the coming five years', it confirms much of what was predicted, from quantum computers and 5G in action to managing cancer, etc. It is also exciting to see that the rapid change in innovative technology will have a major impact in solving some of the world's most pressing problems, such as feeding a global and growing population, improving access to and quality of healthcare, and significantly reducing carbon emissions to arrest the negative effects of climate change.

Ask yourself:
How can I be part of the improvements and the solutions that will take place?
How can I put technology to my own use and possibly my own business?
This kind of question is addressed to you, as you are the young person, you are the entrepreneur, you are the fresh graduate, you are the newly hired employee, you are who you are regardless of what stage and phase of your life you are in at this point.

SHARPEN YOUR KNIFE

There is no doubt that the COVID-19 pandemic has provided a difficult lesson in just how susceptible our world is today to such events, but also with such mega events come mega opportunities.

Having the right mindset will always be your cutting edge in harnessing and creating more solutions.
Regardless of technology itself, you need to be in a position first and

foremost to have sharpened skills, which we discussed in Part One of the book, and this is not simply a one-time exercise, but a continued drive just like brushing your teeth.

Second, you should be able to make some sense of the new reality and where we are heading, with some understanding to be better placed as to where you see yourself within this new reality, and to plug yourself in it while being self-fulfilled and living a meaningful life.

TECH TRENDS

A good place to start is by getting yourself familiar with what's happening as we speak, and what will take place in the coming years and how it will be shaped. You will get to be more familiar with subjects and terms that did not exist a mere short while ago. In his book titled: *Tech Trends in Practice: The 25 Technologies that are Driving the 4th Industrial Revolution* Bernard Marr went to great lengths in describing this subject area. The trends he listed are as follows:

Artificial intelligence (AI) and machine learning;
The Internet of Things (IoT);
Wearables and augmented humans;
Big Data and augmented analytics;
Intelligent spaces and smart places;
Blockchains and distributed ledgers;
Cloud and edge computing;
Digitally extended realities;
Digital twins;
Natural language processing;
Voice interfaces and chatbots;
Computer vision and facial recognition;
Robots and cobots;
Autonomous vehicles;
5G;
Genomics and gene editing;
Machine co-creativity and augmented design;
Digital platforms;
Drones and unmanned aerial vehicles;
Cybersecurity and resilience;
Quantum computing;
Robotic process automation;
Mass personalization and micro-moments;

3D and 4D printing and additive manufacturing; Nanotechnology and materials science.

PUTTING IT ALL TOGETHER

My experience with the corporate world ...

I was caught up in the corporate reality to the point that when I was promoted at a relatively young age in my twenties into senior management and decorated with a C-level title, it felt damn good, and all I wanted was climbing up the ranks and being on top of that ladder! Equally, it blinded me from seeing the bigger picture outside that narrow view. It took many years before establishing my own Coaching and Consulting firm for me to realize that life is short, and living by choice is way more meaningful than living by obligation.

When was the last time you reviewed your own title?

True, we are not all born to be entrepreneurs, founders, co-founders, freelancers, etc., but it is worth it and certainly about time that you took a pit stop to ask yourself a few basic questions:
What is my purpose?
Am I happy?
What do I value most?
How can I belong to the vast and abundant universe beyond the corporate thing?
Am I living by choice? Or by obligation?

As you have no doubt noticed, this book is not about success.
It isn't a pure self-help book.

I am not trying to preach to you.

In essence, it is me sharing with you my essential experiences and learnings.

If practiced and applied, these learnings can provide you with clues to a more meaningful life.
A life that has a sense of purpose.
A life that has some direction and meaning to it.

Happiness is a big word that we all struggle with and find it difficult to achieve in many cases.

I wrote this book in the time of COVID-19, where many things that had value lost it overnight, and many other things that had no value became of prime importance.

I highlighted in previous chapters learnable skills that you can acquire to build yourself. And when you develop these skills, you are then ready and prepared to reach out to the new world or the new ecosystem.

The second part focused on understanding this world and finding your spot in it where you bring relevance and value and self-fulfillment. This book comes as my short answer to the question:

How do you thrive in a changing world?

True, in today's corporate world, titles may be necessary to reflect the designation of what you do in an organization and what your capacity of decision-making is, for example, but equally we know that in a changing world, and an even faster-changing corporate environment, we have a lot to learn in order to evolve and thrive.

When Mahatma Gandhi died, the American journalist Edward R Murrow, broadcasting at the funeral paid this moving tribute:

'The object of this massive tribute died as he had always lived – a private man without wealth, without property, without official title or office. Mahatma Gandhi was not a commander of great armies nor ruler of vast lands. He could boast no scientific achievements or artistic gift. Yet men, governments and dignitaries from all over the world have joined hands today to pay homage to this little brown man in the loincloth who led his country to freedom.'

What does this tell us? And what if we also plug this observation into today's world of learning from Generation Z?

Generation Z are after value, freedom, self-fulfillment, and healthy environments to work in and in which to be productive. According to a *Forbes* article written in September 2019, 'How Generation-Z Will Revolutionize The Workplace', it clearly mentions that they value three things:
1. More work–life balance,
2. Technology, and
3. A good mindset and feedback.

Titles become less relevant and important.

What do Gandhi and ***#GenerationZ*** have in common?
What have we got to learn from a little brown man who held no official title nor an official office and yet inspired and moved the world at large? What do we need to learn from #***GenerationZ***, and what do they and Gandhi have in common to offer for the modern corporate executive in the corporate environment?

It comes as no surprise that there is a significant rise in ***#Entrepreneurship***, as clearly portrayed by the ***#GlobalEntrepreneurshipIndex (#GEI)***, and this is not by coincidence nor by obligation, but by choice.

Entrepreneurs understand perfectly well the common ground between Gandhi and Generation Z. They have enough courage to simply ***be***. They know their passion and they pursue it.

After all, it was Steve Jobs who once said:
'Your time is limited, so don't waste it living someone else's life.

Don't be trapped by dogma – which is living with the results of other people's thinking.

Don't let the **noise** of other's opinions drown out your own inner voice. And most important, have the ***#courage*** **to follow your heart and intuition**.'

A new century requires a new mindset and skills:
Untapped opportunity lies within your own passions and talent potential. If self-belief is your currency, coupled with what Professor Yuval Harari referred to in his book, *21 Lessons for the 21st Century*, whereby he noted that

UNTAPPED OPPORTUNITY LIES WITHIN YOUR OWN PASSIONS AND TALENT POTENTIAL

you would require harnessing what he calls the four Cs – Communication, Collaboration, Critical Thinking, and Creativity – then maybe it is about time that you consider your own passions and potential.

Some of the key trends highlighted when researching the ***#FutureofWork*** are that the world of work is constantly changing faster than ever before and companies must stay abreast of new ***#trends***, as must their employees. Both ***#Technology*** and ***#Globalization*** have created a world where it is possible to work with anyone from anywhere.

There are no limitations, but only ***#SelfLimitingBeliefs.***

You know you've got the talent, you know that you are not satisfied with the way things are done in your environment, so why not be courageous to venture into living a better quality and a more liberating way of life?

Why not consider taking a leap of faith of finding what **you** love – and do it? You are born to be royal, hence living by choice and not by obligation. Take your first step and look at your **#jobTitle**, as you are worth so much more than just that! In the literal meaning of it, all you need to do is learn to be yourself, but with skill.

Why? So **you** can honor yourself and others by creating a positive impact around **you**. My last thought to **you** is this: When in doubt, have faith in yourself; maintain a strong mindset, up-to-date skillset, and always have courage to trust in your own intuition and experience.

WHEN IN DOUBT, HAVE FAITH IN YOURSELF, AND TRUST YOUR INTUITION!

Made in the USA
Las Vegas, NV
20 March 2023

69363983R00072